JANE AUSTEN'S SEWING BOX

CRAFT PROJECTS & STORIES FROM JANE AUSTEN'S NOVELS

JANE AUSTEN'S SEWING BOX

CRAFT PROJECTS & STORIES FROM JANE AUSTEN'S NOVELS

JENNIFER FOREST

MURDOCH BOOKS

contents

Introduction

THE REGENCY WORLD OF JANE AUSTEN'S WOMEN

Jane Austen's novels were set in the late 1700s to early 1800s, the years known as the Regency after the Prince Regent (later George IV).

This world in which Jane Austen and her women lived was characterised by the opposites of consistency and change. The Regency was firmly based in the old world of landed estates and small country towns. However, the new world of the industrial revolution was bringing substantial change, particularly to consumption and class.

For many people in the countryside, such as the family of Harriet Smith's beau Robert Martin in *Emma*, life continued very much as it had done so for the last century. Members of the family were agricultural workers for the local estate or worked in their home-based enterprise, for example as a dairy farmer, spinner or weaver. Each family provided their own food from their poultry, vegetable garden and, if income allowed, cows, sheep or goats. Any extra produce was sold or traded locally and the profit used to buy necessities, or luxuries like sugar and tea. Members of the gentry, such as the religious parson and small landowners like Mr Bennet in *Pride and Prejudice,* bridged the gap between the rural workers and the wealthy families of the local estates. Political and economic power was based on grand estates like Pemberley or large ones like Donwell Abbey and Norland Park. Such estates defined the character of the area and provided employment for workers and, through charity, a safety net for the poor and destitute.

'he [Mr Darcy] *is the best landlord, and the best master,' said she, 'that ever lived'.*
Pride and Prejudice

By the Regency Era, the new world of the industrial revolution was already changing Britain. London, the largest city in the country, was the hub of the emerging British empire. The ports of Bristol and Liverpool were growing wealthy on the back of trade. A key link in the slave trade to the Americas, they received the return trade of sugar and rum from the West Indies and cotton from the Americas.

Sir Thomas was indeed the life of the party... his business in Antigua had latterly been prosperously rapid, and he came directly from Liverpool
Mansfield Park

Improvements in agricultural technology allowed one worker to feed himself and two others, freeing up a rural population to take up regular work in the new factories. Textile mills were already appearing alongside waterways around the country. Home-based enterprises in spun yarn, woven cloth and knitted stockings were replaced by these mills, which used machinery to produce huge volumes of cloth. By the end of the

Regency Era the growth in the number of textile factories was so great that Britain had become a major exporter of cotton cloth and yarn to the rest of the world.

A system of water canals allowed the abundant products of the industrial revolution—manufactured cloth, agricultural produce and a range of consumer items like furniture and porcelain—to move around Britain. The development of a good road network, the best since Roman Britain, meant that for the first time Jane Austen and her women could easily travel to Bath, Lyme and London, although it was a bumpy ride in a wooden carriage.

Wealthy, landed families who relied on agriculture, like Mr Darcy in *Pride and Prejudice* and Mr Knightley in *Emma,* continued to play a vital role in feeding the nation and providing employment. However, war with revolutionary (and later Napoleonic) France and trade with Europe and the Americas, opened up new opportunities for other classes. The rising fortunes of naval officers like Captain Wentworth in *Persuasion* and traders like the Coles in *Emma* meant that they now had money once confined in the hands of the upper classes. Captain Wentworth's assets of £25,000, or £1250 a year when invested in government bonds, places him in the same league as status conscious Emma Woodhouse, with her £30,000, or £1500 a year.

Captain Wentworth, with five-and-twenty thousand pounds, and as high in his profession as merit and activity could place him, was no longer nobody.

Persuasion

Britain was now manufacturing high-quality goods like printed fabrics, porcelain, furniture, industrial tools and machinery, instead of relying on high-quality furniture and fashion imported from Europe. Speciality stores in the major cities provided off-the-rack bonnets and hats, cloaks, shoes and gloves. Salesmen travelled the countryside carrying printed catalogues with drawings of their wares such as side tables, cabinets, porcelain, candlesticks and swatches of fabrics, wallpaper and paint. Advertisements in newspapers heralded the arrival of new fabrics and prints in city-based shops that also provided, in many cases, a mail-order service. Paper dolls from France, dressed in replicas of the latest dresses, and fashion magazines encouraged men and women alike to remain up-to-date with new trends.

Dress was her passion. She had a most harmless delight in being fine

Northanger Abbey

Such abundance though did not come without its challenges. Not all classes enjoyed the new wealth and the poor were the hardest hit when the economy came under immense pressure from war with France. The illness and hunger born of the poverty that defined the lives of factories workers were already topics of heated public debate. Then, in an attempt to weaken Britain, Napoleon blocked British trade with Europe. The result was high levels of unemployment for textile workers as the demand for British cloth plummeted. Artificially high food prices and reduced wages lead to riots and marches, including attacks by disgruntled textile workers known as Luddites who were being replaced by new mechanised looms. It is not surprising then that in such a climate of unrest that, in *Northanger Abbey*, Catherine Morland's excited anticipation about the release of a new gothic novel from London publishers is misinterpreted by Eleanor Tilney as news of further riots in the city.

'A particular friend of mine had an account of it in a letter from London yesterday. It is to be uncommonly dreadful. I shall expect murder and every thing of the kind.'

'You speak with astonishing composure! But I hope your friend's accounts have been exaggerated;—and if such a design is known beforehand, proper measures will undoubtedly be taken by government to prevent its coming to effect'.

Catherine and Eleanor, Northanger Abbey

Women of the upper classes were largely confined to a private world, with little scope for a public political or economic role. It was their husbands, fathers and brothers who were the Members of Parliament, traders and professionals. Paid employment was only for women of lower classes who had to work out of necessity. Yet women in this private world worked at home and held significant management roles. In any household of some means there were staff and food supplies to manage—sometimes a kitchen garden, dairy or farm—children's education to supervise and regular chores such as washing the laundry and making the men's clothes. In a grand estate like Pemberley, the mistress had a considerable management role, with a large budget, many staff and significant charity work to manage.

'They were all warm in their admiration; and at that moment she [Elizabeth] felt that to be mistress of Pemberley might be something!'

Pride and Prejudice

Throughout the era, there are examples of women from across the classes exercising some economic control over their lives. The textile industry provided opportunities in the new factories for working women; factory work was initially seen as suitable for women and children. Female mantua-makers (dressmakers), embroiderers, fabric print designers, shoemakers and milliners worked for others, operated from home or established stores in villages and cities. The other main area providing work for women was in nursing or educating children. For example the role of governess, while often scorned, allowed some options for an educated woman of some standing.

The respectable choice though, for women of the upper classes, was essentially a life of economic dependency. A spinster with no fortune relied on her father or brothers for an income and a home. The alternative of marriage, which secured a home, was not always an appealing prospect in a time of high mortality rates from childbirth. An inheritance provided women with some choice, though few property rights, allowing a trader's daughter like Augusta Hawkins to marry a clergyman (Mr Elton) in *Emma,* or an heiress with £50,000 like Sophia Grey to choose her husband Willoughby in *Sense and Sensibility.*

'Fifty thousand pounds! And by all accounts it won't come before it's wanted; for they say he is all to pieces. No wonder! Dashing about with his curricle and hunters!'
Sense and Sensibility

JANE AUSTEN'S WOMEN AND THEIR CRAFT

Sewing, either as plain or fancy needlework, was such an all-consuming and important part of a woman's day that it was called 'women's work'. Such work provided by women was a valuable economic contribution, essential to clothe the family, keep a house warm and support the poor. It was also important as a creative outlet in the form of decorative art.

Most women spent their work time on plain sewing. It was an era when thrift was a virtue and for many women living in the country, a trip to a major town or city was required to purchase the latest fabric and yarns. While gentlemen might purchase a new coat each year from a tailor, the women of the family made their shirts, cravats and nightwear and took pride in cutting a piece of linen to minimise waste. Women likewise may have purchased a ready-made bonnet but it was usual practice to select dress fabric they desired and then take it to a dressmaker to be made up.

Women altered their own dresses to fit changing body shape and to keep up with fashion. For example, adding flounces or ribbon trimming along the hem as more lavish decoration became fashionable. A dress would be re-used, cut up for a cloak or bodice piece or turned into clothes for the children. Household linen like sheets, towels and pillowcases were often made in the home as well. The importance of rugs for the floor and quilts for the beds should not be forgotten in houses warmed only by fires in each room.

Mrs Norris began scolding 'That is a very foolish trick, Fanny, to be idling away all the evening upon a sofa. Why can not you come and sit here and employ yourself as we do? If you have no work of your own, I can supply you from the poor basket.'

Mansfield Park

Women's work also played an important role in supporting the poor families of a rural area. Sharing the wealth of the upper classes through charity like this was an important safety net to protect the poor from complete destitution. A virtuous wealthy woman would pay particular attention to making clothes for the poor, such as a set of baby linen for village women or mending old nightwear and undergarments as gifts for servants. Such gifts of charity, in addition to food, particularly when village families were ill, could mean the difference to a young child's survival.

Needlework and the other crafts and arts like drawing, netting, painting, filigree and knitting provided an important creative opportunity for women. Wealthy women were expected to perfect their skill in fancy work such as embroidery and carpet work, and in drawing or painting. While plain sewing was kept from sight, completed within the family circle only, fancy work was performed in the company of visitors and guests. It was a sign of the skill and leisure time enjoyed by the women of the family, wealthy enough not to need its women to work on menial tasks, or at least not to knit their own stockings.

'I am quite in raptures with her [Georgiana] *beautiful little design for a table, and I think it infinitely superior to Miss Grantley's'*
Miss Bingley to Darcy, Pride and Prejudice

The Regency Era was a time of enthusiastic appreciation of design in all forms—dress, architecture, interiors, furniture, wallpaper and fabric. With such a flourish of interest in design, particularly interiors, there were opportunities for women to exercise their design talents and technical skill in their chosen craft. Inspiration was drawn most often from nature but also from the design themes of the era—medieval and gothic, Chinese, Indian, Moorish and Classical Rome and Greece. New printing techniques and colours presented exciting design options—a remnant of brilliantly printed fabric or silk thread could be worked into a design. Craftspeople then, as now, experienced the same creative impulse and sense of satisfaction or fulfilment when they turned a needle to a new piece of embroidery, sewed a novel trim to a bonnet or applied a brush to a blank canvas.

The house was handsome, and handsomely fitted up; and the young ladies were immediately put in possession of a very comfortable apartment... and over the mantle piece still hung a landscape in coloured silks

Sense and Sensibility

Set within a historical context Jane Austen's references to craft in her novels were well recognised by her readers. They knew what 'work' meant when she has Anne Elliott and her sister Mary sitting at work in the window in *Persuasion*. They knew that painting transparencies and netting purses were artistic crazes of the time, popular amongst a certain wealthy and leisured set of young women, like Isabella Thorpe who nets in *Northanger Abbey*, and the Bertrams in *Mansfield Park* in their fickle enthusiasm for transparencies.

In a world where diligence and application to a woman's work is widely admired as a virtue, Jane Austen also sends clear signals about the character of her women through craft. In *Mansfield Park* Elinor Dashwood, unlike her sister Marianne, is a diligent worker and an accomplished designer and painter. By contrast, the Bertram sisters pay less than diligent attention to their education. Fanny Price's East Room is home to the cast aside creative endeavours of her relatives.

...a faded footstool of Julia's work, too ill done for the drawing room... a collection of family profiles thought unworthy of anywhere else...

It is a sign of Fanny Price's strength of character, in contrast to her wayward cousins, that she is constantly assisting her aunt with her embroidery.

'Had you seen her this morning, Mary' he [Henry Crawford] continued, 'attending with such ineffable sweetness and patience to all the demands of her aunt's stupidity, working with her, and for her, her colour beautifully heightened as she leant over the work...'

Mansfield Park

Emma Woodhouse, resplendent in her fortune, family and status, devotes minimal effort to perfecting the usual accomplishments. She identifies women's work as the lot of older women, and like her visits to those less fortunate than herself, sees it as a little unnecessary.

While craft is not often associated with Elizabeth Bennet, she is one last example of the way in which Jane Austen uses craft as a signal to her readers. Despite Elizabeth's horror at her friend Charlotte's pragmatic decision to marry Mr Collins, she readily visits her and recognises the value of a morning of companionable work with her friend. Elizabeth is also only too aware of the value of women's work in providing her with an acceptable distraction in times of social need, such as when she does not wish to engage Darcy in conversation.

Elizabeth said as little either as civility would allow, and sat down again to her work, with an eagerness which it did not often command. She had ventured only one glance at Darcy.

Pride and Prejudice

Women's work permeates Jane Austen's novels, as it did in the real lives of Regency women. Set within a historical context, Regency women's work is seen as one part of their valuable economic contribution to the household and community. In a time when few women were recognised as professional artists in their own right, the skills of sewing, netting, knitting, drawing and painting provided women with an avenue for artistic expression, in the creation of items of utility and beauty.

Materials and tools

FABRICS AND THREADS

Four main fabrics were used during the Regency Era—silk, wool, linen and cotton.

SILK

Silk thread is unwound from the cocoons of the silk worm and then twisted into yarn or woven into cloth. Silk is strong with a very fine, gleaming appearance. It is warmer than cotton and wears well throughout the seasons. Britain had a silk manufacturing industry built on the skills of the French Huguenot (protestant) refugees. France, the European centre of dress silk, and Italy, which specialised in silk furnishings, were also sources of silk, although the supply of European silk was at the mercy of legislation to protect the domestic industry and war with France. Silk fabric was often exquisitely embroidered with silk thread for dress fabric.

WOOL

Wool is soft, warm and malleable. The yarn can be manipulated in a variety of ways to make cloth—woven, knitted or felted. Worsted wool, with the long fibres combed together, is strong and smooth and produces a fine woven cloth suitable for clothing. Worsted yarn was used for carpet work, crewel work and knitting. Prior to the rise of cotton,

Britain dominated the raw wool and fine woollen cloth trade, a key British export to Europe.

LINEN

Linen is a very strong, crisp and smooth fabric used for clothing, furnishings and sail cloth. Made from the fibres of the flax plant, linen cloth in Britain was mostly imported from Germany and Ireland. Irish linen developed a reputation as a very fine cloth and was known as 'the Irish'. Linen was often interwoven with cotton and formed a good base for printing. Linen thread was used in embroidery such as white work.

COTTON

Cotton, made from the fibres of the cotton plant, is a strong, versatile fabric, which absorbs paints and dyes well. In this era Britain emerged as the world leader in the manufacture of woven and printed cotton cloth. Printed cottons initially came from India but developments in printing allowed Britain to dominate the European and American markets. The old method was to use hand-held wood blocks to stamp the fabric with paint. Hand painted embellishments were then added to create a multi-coloured design. The invention of copperplate printing allowed single colour, fine-lined pictorial prints to become widespread. By the end of the Regency Era roller printing, using engraved copper rollers, allowed designs in multiple colours to be printed on long lengths of fabric. Chintz was a popular cotton fabric that benefited from these developments. It was prized for dress making with its many printed colours, which imitated embroidered silk. Muslin was also characteristic of the era, popular for the soft gentle lines that the open, transparent and soft weave created. Printed cottons made colour affordable to more and more people—cochineal pinks and reds, buff, gold and vivid yellows, purples and orange, and many shades of greens and blue.

Unlike cotton, other materials like coloured paper and glass were not yet mass-produced, making crafts using such items comparatively more expensive. Soaking, pounding and moulding cotton and linen fibres from rags was the method of making paper during the Regency Era. Wood pulp and straw may have been added to the mix but wood pulp was not yet used as the base of paper. Printers and stationers sold a range of paper directly to the public.

Artist's colour men, the forerunner of the modern art store, sold paper, canvas, brushes, pencils, water-colour paints and a range of oil paints. Artist's colour men often produced their own paints, drawing on their own experiments with different combinations and additives to perfect their colour selection. Pencils were made from graphite with additives like glue and charcoal or dust rolled together into sticks and then placed in a metal or wooden case.

TOOLS

As sewing machines were not available until the mid-1800s, all Regency clothing, craft, furnishing and industrial items like sail cloth were sewn by hand. Scissors had existed for many centuries, but cast iron pivoted handle and blade scissors were mass-produced for the first time in the Regency Era. Pins and sewing needles were produced by hand from iron wire. Many sewing tools were carved from wood, such as thread winders (also made in shell or bone), which held valuable silk, linen and cotton threads for embroidery as thread was not sold on reels during this period. A knotting shuttle, a smooth, elongated oval with a centre anchor to wind the thread was also made from bone or shell.

Netting tools, the gauge and the shuttle, were also often made from bone or shell. The gauge could also be a smoothed length of wood in the desired width. The shuttle or netting needle was a thin, long piece of metal with open, hooked ends to hold the thread.

The craft projects included are modelled on Regency examples and research but with the modern craftsperson in mind. For example, reference is made to using a sewing machine to make a project. Many a Regency woman would have appreciated a sewing machine to make the many shirts and bed linen she was required to finish for her family.

Each project is also given a skill level. The skill level is based on two factors—technical craft skill and time to complete the project. For example, a beginner level project requires a little knowledge of the craft skill and can be completed fairly quickly. Whereas an intermediate to advanced project requires some knowledge of the craft skill, or at least a willingness to try, and will take a good block of time to complete.

Letter case

Novels *Northanger Abbey, Emma, Pride & Prejudice,
Persuasion and Sense & Sensibility*

Improvements in literacy and the postal system encouraged letter writing to flourish during the Regency Era. The growth of a literate population echoed the rising consumer power of the gentry and middle class, keen to educate their children. Young men could now seek livelihoods outside agriculture. The increasingly respectable professions of law and banking demanded literate staff, as did many other emerging areas of employment. Likewise, a well-educated woman was expected to manage her own household's staff, supplies and associated finances, requiring a degree of literacy and numeracy previously unknown.

Meanwhile the improved roads, the best since the Romans laid roads in Britain, allowed a postal network to develop across the country. The postal system was so efficient by this time, that Jane Austen's letter to publishers Crosby & Co in London of the 5th April 1809, seeking the fate of *Susan* (later called *Northanger Abbey*), could be sent from Southampton, received, and a reply written, by the 8th April 1809.

The recipient paid the cost of postage based on the number of sheets of paper and the distance travelled, and could refuse a letter if they wished. As envelopes were not yet in common use, the sheet of paper was folded and secured with a wax seal, and the address written on the outside. The imposition of cost on the recipient also encouraged letter writers to seek a frank from a local Member of Parliament or to enlist travelling friends and family to deliver letters for them.

Letter writing was the only way to keep families informed of children's progress or the comings and goings of family members. With many men serving in the navy or the army during the Napoleonic Wars, letter writing connected families throughout years of separation. Jane and Cassandra Austen wrote to each other on a regular basis when apart and visiting family members. Jane Austen delighted in Cassandra's letters, commending her skill in 1796.

'My dearest Cassandra, The letter which I have this moment received from you has diverted me beyond moderation. I could die of laughter at it, as they used to say at school. You are indeed the finest comic writer of the present age.'

Letter writing was not without its rules and boundaries—Jane Austen illustrated both in her novels. Women regularly wrote to each other regardless of whether they were related by birth or marriage. Letters between brothers and sisters were acceptable, as is seen when James Morland communicates his broken engagement to his sister Catherine in *Northanger Abbey*. It was, however, very uncommon for a woman to write to an unrelated man unless on business matters or as his fiancée. In *Sense and Sensibility*, both Elinor Dashwood and her younger sister Margaret assume that Marianne is engaged to Willoughby because of their frequent letter writing and Marianne's gift of a lock of her hair to Willoughby. He recounts to Elinor how his fiancée found Marianne's letters.

'her three notes—unluckily they were all in my pocketbook, or I should have denied their existence, and hoarded them forever—I was forced to put them up, and could not even kiss them. And the lock of hair—that too, I had always carried about me in the same pocket-book, which was now searched by madam with the most ingratiating virulence...'
Sense and Sensibility

In an era when unrelated men and women did not generally write to each other, it is a sign of both Darcy's and Captain Wentworth's depth of anxiety that they resort to letters. In *Pride and Prejudice* Darcy takes the bold step of writing to Elizabeth in response to her claims of ill treatment of her sister Jane and Mr Wickham when she refuses his first proposal.

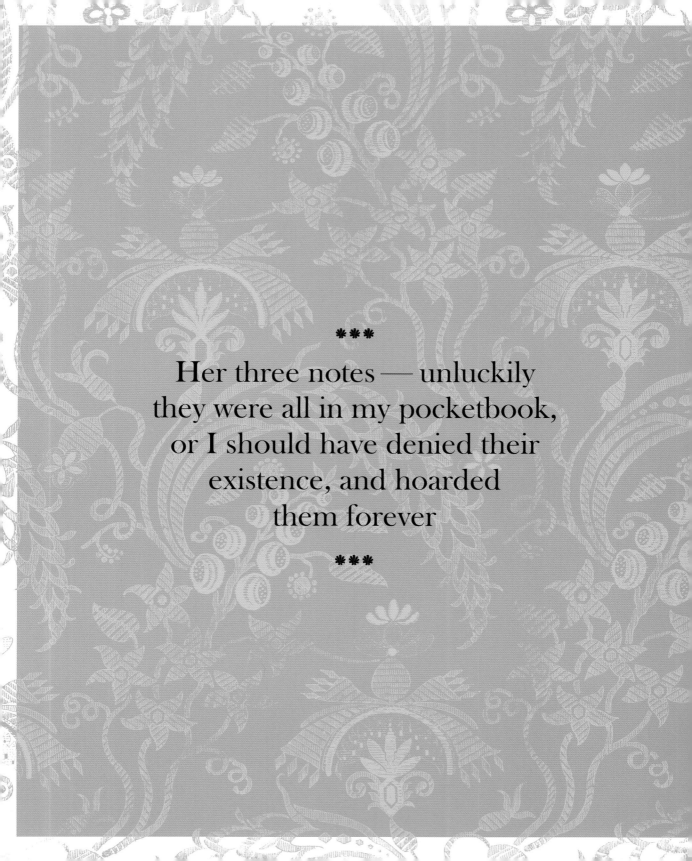

❋❋❋

Her three notes — unluckily
they were all in my pocketbook,
or I should have denied their
existence, and hoarded
them forever

❋❋❋

'Be not alarmed, Madam, on receiving this letter, by the apprehension of its containing any repetition of those sentiments, or renewal of those offers, which were last night so disgusting to you... Two offences of a very different nature, and by no means of equal magnitude, you last night laid to my charge...'

Pride and Prejudice

Likewise in *Persuasion* Captain Wentworth writes a letter to Anne Elliot that he can only leave on a table in the hope that she will pick it up. Upon overhearing Anne and Captain Harville discussing who loves the longest—men or women—he offers anew, evidence of his enduring attachment.

'I can no listen no longer in silence. I must speak to you by such means as are within my reach. You pierce my soul. I am half agony, half hope...'

Persuasion

The skill of writing was also deployed to record the particulars of daily life—a pocket book was a valuable accessory. Both men and women carried pocket books, like Willoughby's, which was a small lined book that could be a diary or a notebook. It was a useful item to record lists, recipes, shopping expenses or upcoming events. Mr Elton in *Emma* uses his pocket book 'to make a memorandum in his pocket-book: it was about spruce-beer. Mr Knightley had been telling him something about brewing spruce-beer and he wanted to put it down'. Women also used pocket books. Isabellla Thorpe keeps a list of horrid gothic thrillers for the two girls to read after Catherine has finished *The Mysteries of Udolpho*.

'I will read you their names directly; here they are in my pocketbook. Castle of Wolfenbach, Clermont, Mysterious Warnings, Necromancer of the Black Forest, Midnight Bell, Orphan of the Rhine and horrid Mysteries. Those will last us some time.'

Northanger Abbey

A pocket book was small enough to slip into a coat or jacket pocket. Alternatively, they were kept in a wallet-like case, called a pocket or letter case, usually made from leather or fabric. A letter case was also used to hold letters and money. Pencils accompanied the pocket book, either attached to the book or secured in the letter case. Graphite with additives like glue and charcoal or dust were rolled together into sticks and then placed in a metal or wooden case—not quite the convenient wooden pencil of today.

Letter case

MATERIALS

* 50 cm of printed cotton
* 50 cm of firm interfacing
* 1 m of velvet ribbon (1 cm wide)
* 1 m of satin ribbon (0.5 cm wide) and two beads
* Metal clasp (in two parts)
* Matching sewing thread
* Notebook (8 x 11 cm)
* Pencil (10 cm)

TOOLS

* Sewing needle/sewing machine
* Tape measure
* Scissors
* Pin
* Iron

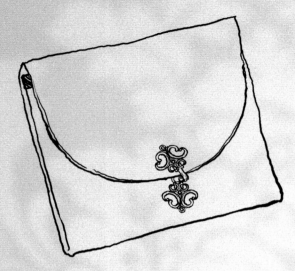

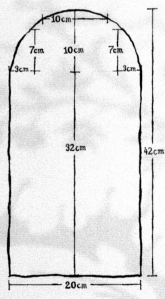

diagram 1

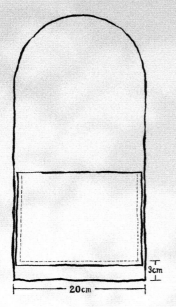

diagram 2

INSTRUCTIONS

1. Cut two pieces of the printed cotton for the front and back panels and one piece of the firm interfacing. Pieces measure 42 x 20 cm with a curved 10 cm starting at 32 cm up on the length (Diagram 1).

2. Cut one pocket piece of 15 x 20 cm from the printed cotton.

3. Iron under a 1 cm hem around all four sides of the pocket piece. Stitch only along the top edge.

4. Pin the pocket to the right side of one panel piece 3 cm up from the base, keeping the ironed hem in place. Stitch around three sides securing the pocket to the panel (Diagram 2).

5. With right sides of the printed cotton together, stitch the two panel pieces and interfacing together. Leave the base open. The curved edge of the lid will need to be clipped to ensure a smooth edge. To make this clipped curve, after the seam has been stitched, make small cuts on the curves of the lid just to the stitch line.

6. Turn the case the right way out and iron under the base edge into a neat seam line. Stitch into place.

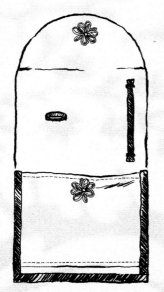

diagram 3

7. Using the velvet ribbon, decorate the inside of the case as desired. The satin ribbon can be used to create multiples of figure eights and stitched in the centre with the bead sewn on top.

8. Stitch at the top and bottom of a 14 cm piece of velvet ribbon along the right hand side edge, 3 cm in from the edge. This becomes the loop to secure the pocketbook. Stitch a 2 cm loop of ribbon next to the notebook which secures the pencil (Diagram 3).

9. Attach one part of the clasp to the outside of the curved lid and the other part to the outside base to close the case.

Linen

Novels *Mansfield Park, Northanger Abbey and Emma*

❋ ❋ ❋

'My dear Catherine, I am afraid you are growing quite a fine lady. I do not know when poor Richard's cravats would be done, if he had no friend but you. Your head runs too much upon Bath, but there is a time for everything—a time for balls and plays, and a time for work'.

Northanger Abbey

Crisp, white breathable linen was the favoured material, until it was replaced with cotton, for shirts, underclothes and household items. Made from the flax plant, linen cloth in Britain was imported from Germany and particularly Ireland. The spinning, weaving and dyeing of linen was based in the cottages of Ireland—all members of the family would make up the cloth pieces for sale. Irish linen developed a reputation as a very fine cloth and was so common in 18th century Britain that the cloth became known as the Irish.

Linen was usually sold in lengths to the consumer who purchased as many yards as needed to make up their shirts or underclothes. In major towns, linen-drapers specialised in linen cloth, while silk and wool had their own speciality stores. In smaller towns, linen was sold by an all-purpose fabric store that stocked a range of fabrics and haberdashery items, such as Ford's in *Emma*.

Particularly in rural areas, travelling salesman known as Scotchmen (though they weren't necessary from Scotland) had yards of linen and ready-made items available. In 1798 Jane Austen purchased a number of items from such a salesman.

'The Overton Scotchman has been kind enough to rid me of some of my money, in exchange for six shifts and four pair of stockings. The Irish is not so fine as I should like it; but as I gave as much money for it as I intended, I have no reason to complain. It cost me 3s. 6d. per yard. It is rather finer, however, than our last, and not so harsh a cloth'.

The women of the family turned the yards of linen into nightwear, shirts and cravats needed by their men. In *Mansfield Park*, when Fanny Price has returned to her family in Portsmouth, she sews the linen her brother Sam needs to take with him before he leaves for his ship.

Fanny was very anxious to be useful and therefore set about working for Sam immediately and by working early and late, with perseverance and great dispatch, did so much, that the boy was shipped off at last, with more than half his linen ready.

Mansfield Park

Both Cassandra and Jane Austen made their brother's shirts. In 1796 while visiting her older brother Edward Austen (later Knight) she wrote 'We are very busy making Edward's shirts and I am proud to say I am the neatest worker of the Party'. In 1799, they made their younger brother Charles' shirts which are then sent to Charles in 'half-dozens as they are finished'.

Like women's fashion, gentlemen's clothes during the Regency Era were also transformed by a move to simplicity of clothing and appearance. Typical daywear was a great coat made from wool, a valuable item for men riding on the outside of coaches or on a horse. The thickness of the wool, its full length and the multiple layers of capes on the shoulders kept them dry in the wet and cold. Men also had their own set of accessories to complement daywear and keep out the cold, particularly leather gloves, wool or felted hats and button-up knee-high boots.

***

... but there is a time for everything—a time for balls and plays, and a time for work

***

The loose fitting trouser was not yet widespread so most men wore either cream-coloured knee breeches with stockings and shoes or the close fitting pantaloon with boots. A dark-coloured frock coat was the fashionable item, with long tails, usually double-breasted and in blue or black. Underneath this was a waistcoat, if expense allowed, in a contrasting colour such as red or embroidered. An under-waistcoat provided additional warmth and colour. The jacket and waistcoat were low collared to allow the striking whiteness of the linen shirt and cravat to be visible.

George 'Beau' Brummell, leader of men's fashion and confidant of the Prince Regent, sponsored the crisp, clean white shirt and cravat, turning the cravat knot and ruffles into an art form. At a time when bathing daily was not common, he also championed personal hygiene, taking great care in his daily toilette and favouring a modern style of short-cropped hair.

A fine cravat was a statement of crispness and cleanliness, a pure white piece of ironed and starched cloth. It was folded from a triangle or square of white muslin, cotton or linen. The cravat was folded into a band wrapped around the neck with the ends tied into a knot at the front. Alternatively a triangle of fabric could be tucked into the front of the shirt and then the remaining fabric wrapped around the neck with the loose ends finishing at the front to form an elaborate knot and ruffle with the triangle.

Many household items like tablecloths, towels, sheets and pillowcases were usually made from linen. In expectation of marriage a girl and her family would sew such items and a set of baby clothes, forming a valuable gift for the setting up of her own household. Gifts of baby linen, such as that sent from Mansfield Park to Mrs Price on the birth of her ninth child would have included caps, nightdresses and sheets for the baby.

While the mens' cravats and shirts were made from a finely spun and woven linen, a coarser and stiffer linen was suited to hard wearing items like bedsheets and pillowcases. While the virtue of frugality is often associated with Victorian times, being clever with a piece of cloth was just as important in the Regency. Cloth was expensive and not always easy to obtain, particular in rural areas, so cutting out pieces for shirts or household items minimised wastage.

Pillowcases

MATERIALS (to make 2 bed pillowcases)

* 1 x 1.5 m of pure white, heavy
  duty linen (such as a shirting linen)
* Matching sewing thread
* 4 m of cotton tape
* 1 m of cotton torchon lace (25 mm wide)
* 1 m of silk ribbon (3 mm wide)

TOOLS

* Sewing needle or sewing machine
* Fabric scissors
* Pin
* Iron
* Spray bottle of water
* Tape measure
* Safety pin

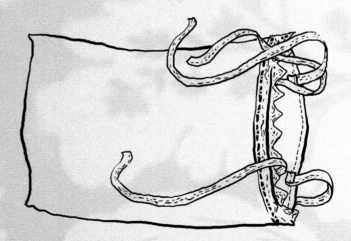

INSTRUCTIONS

1. Fold material in half and cut two rectangles on the fold – 70 x 44 cm. Follow steps 2–7 for each pillowcase.

2. Using a French seam (Diagram 1), hem each long side, finishing 4 cm from the top edge.

3. Iron and pin under the two raw edges at the top of the pillowcase. Use a small rolled hem (see Diagram 1 in Cravat).

4. Cut four lengths of the cotton tape of 40 cm each. Fold over one end twice. Pin this folded tape edge 10cm in from the side of the pillowcase. Pin onto the underneath of the rolled hem. Sew into place. Stitch another piece of cotton tape 10 cm in from the other side of the pillowcase.

5. Turn and repeat for the other edge of the pillowcase top. There should now be four ties on the pillowcase. Edge each end of the cotton ties by folding over twice and sewing into place.

6. Thread the cotton torchon lace with the 3 mm silk ribbon through the lace holes. Attaching the safety pin to the end of the ribbon provides a firm grip on the thin silk ribbon.

French seam

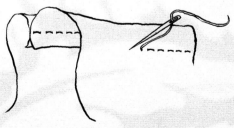

Diagram 1

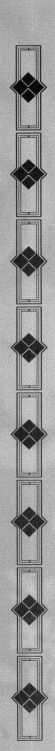

7.   Pin the cotton torchon lace to the edge of the pillow and stitch into place.

To make a French seam:

1.   With the wrong sides together, sew a straight running stitch close to the edge.

2.   Turn the piece so the wrong sides are now facing out and form a crease to cover this first straight row of stitches.

3.   Make a second row of stitches away from the creased edge with the first row of stitches hidden in the middle (Diagram 1).

Oriental   Mathematical   Osbaldeston

Napoleon   American   Mail Coach

Trone d Amour   Irish   Ball Room

Horse Collar   Hunting   Maharatta

Gordian Knot   Barrel Knot

Way of Folding

Cravat

MATERIALS

* 1 x 1.5 m of pure white, fine linen
  (such as handkerchief linen)
* Matching sewing thread

TOOLS

* Sewing needle or sewing machine
* Fabric scissors
* Pin
* Iron
* Spray bottle of water
* Tape measure

INSTRUCTIONS

1. Measure a triangle 148 x 95 x 95 cm and cut.

2. Turn over a rolled hem along each of the three sides. To make a rolled hem (Diagram 1), fold over 1 cm of hem and iron into place, roll this 1 cm edge over again tucking the raw edge underneath, iron and pin into place. Keep each triangle point neat, ensuring no raw fabric is visible.

3. With a neat backstitch, or plain stitch on the sewing machine, stitch hem into place.

4. Dampen triangle before ironing each hem and the body of the triangle.

5. With the long side of the triangle at the top, fold over 12 cm and iron into place. Fold this 12 cm band over two more times (Diagram 2), ironing into place each time. The cravat can then be worn with smooth edges out, raw edges wrapped around the neck with a knot tied at the front.

Rolled hem

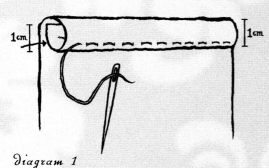

1cm   1cm

diagram 1

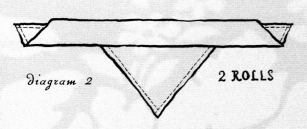

diagram 2   2 ROLLS

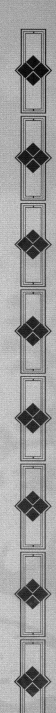

Technique Sewing and
Embroidery
Level Intermediate

Workbag

Novels *Sense and Sensibility, Persuasion,*
Northanger Abbey

❋ ❋ ❋

The Regency Era saw a vast improvement in the quality of the roads, allowing people to travel, for shopping, holidays, health or to visit family and friends, in unprecedented numbers. The seven-hour return journey to Lyme in *Persuasion* to visit acquaintances and take the sea air, or the attempt in *Northanger Abbey* to view Blaize Castle (15 miles away) in an afternoon, were now commonplace possibilities.

Yet travel was not without its problems. Death and injury from carriages overturned on the poor roads were still common. Working class women could travel in the public coach alone, but respectable women could never travel alone. Regardless of their means of transport, they always required company—preferably a male relative, or if that was not possible, a female companion or servant. In *Northanger Abbey*, General Tilney's return of Catherine to her family, by public coach and without a companion, was well understood by Regency readers to be a slight. A constant theme of the correspondence between Jane and Cassandra Austen is reliance on their brothers to escort them to their destination. In 1811 when their elder brother Edward is required to escort Cassandra from Godmersham Park to London, Jane comments that she is '...very glad to hear of his kind promise of bringing you to town'.

Visits with families, friends and acquaintances were governed by strict protocols of etiquette. A long visit of several weeks or months was acceptable given the distances and difficulties of travel. Many single women played a valuable caring and supportive role to relatives, attending the sick, assisting in childbirth and caring for babies in their first three months. It was also useful for a widowed brother to be able to call upon his unmarried sisters to help care for the children and run the house. Long visits of several weeks to good friends was appropriate but it was unlikely, due to the cost of hosting guests, for the visit to extend into months.

Shorter morning visits, which didn't require extensive travel, formed a key part of the daily ritual. Visits to friends and acquaintances, unless invited otherwise, were strictly confined to the morning. A late breakfast, and dinner between 6 to 8pm, meant that morning visits were commonly accepted as meaning between 12 to 3pm. A visiting card was left with the host's servant who would confirm with the family if they were 'at home', that is, happy to receive a visit. The strict protocols of recognition, dependent on social status, meant that it was perfectly acceptable for a family to refuse a visitor if they were unknown or of dubious standing. Likewise a visitor could indicate that they only wished to stay for a short visit by remaining clothed in their outer wear, their coats, spencers and pelisses. To ensure offence was not taken, a short stay had to be at least fifteen minutes. It was inevitable that the host family would feel obliged to return a visit, ensuring a cycle of visits and return visits.

When visiting with good friends, it was possible for women to spend several hours in companionable discussion and needlework. It was not at all acceptable to be mending, knitting stockings or making clothes for the family or the poor. For either the host or the guest, the etiquette of visiting meant that only fancy work, such as fine embroidery, was appropriate in company. The fancy work becomes a topic of discussion, and an opportunity to demonstrate skill and productivity. The work bag was a perfectly acceptable and useful item to take travelling and visiting with family and friends.

A work bag housed all the materials needed for a project and may have also contained the huswife (see page 101), which held all the tools and threadcases. Work bags, for visiting, were often elaborately decorated with embroidery and a knotted fringe. They could also be relatively plain if made by young girls, in school or at home, learning their first stitches.

When the Miss Steeles and Miss Dashwoods visit Lady Middleton in *Sense and Sensibility* they bring their workbags.

She [Lady Middleton] *saw with maternal complacency all the impertinent incroachments and mischievous tricks to which her cousins submitted. She saw their sashes untied, their hair*

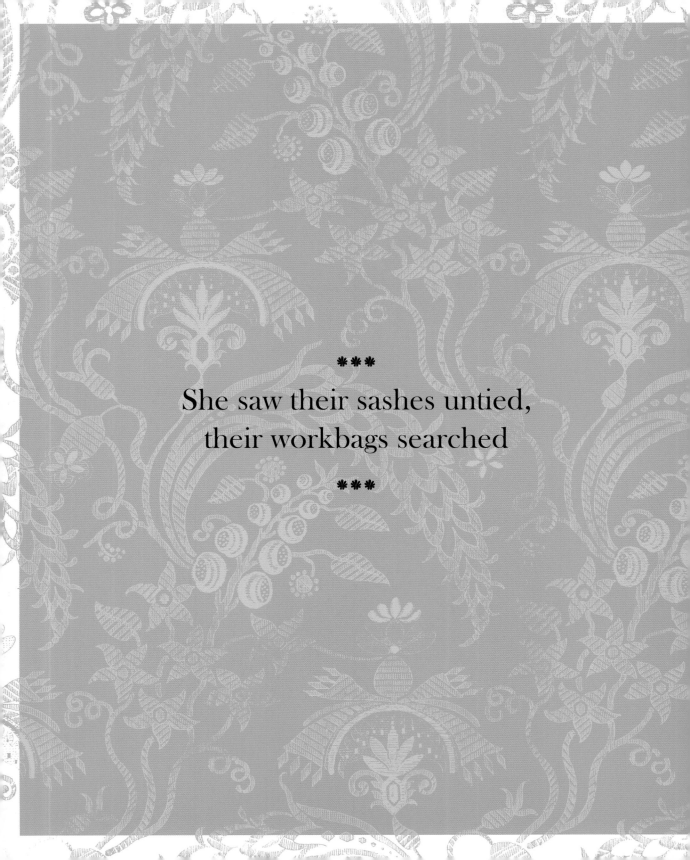

***

She saw their sashes untied,
their workbags searched

***

pulled about their ears, their work bags searched, and their knives and scissors stolen away, and felt no doubt of its being a reciprocal enjoyment. It suggested no other surprise than that Elinor and Marianne should sit composedly by, without claiming a share in what was passing.

Sense and Sensibility

❀ ❀ ❀

Workbag

Finished size: Small work bag—25 x 36 cm,
Finished size: Large work bag—33 x 40 cm

MATERIALS

* 50 cm of white silk (for a small workbag)
  or 50 cm of cotton (for a large work bag)
* Dark green, medium pink and maroon silk
  embroidery thread (Madeira Silk No: 0811-13,
  1314-L11 & 0812-12 used in the white workbag
  pictured on page 62)
* 2 m of satin ribbon per workbag
* Sewing thread

TOOLS

* Sewing needle or sewing machine
* Fabric scissors
* Transfer pen /pencil
* Embroidery design
* Embroidery hoop

Embroidery design
Enlarge by 250%

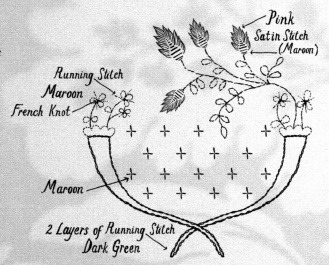

INSTRUCTIONS

1. Cut two panels of 33 x 43 cm (or 38 x 48 cm for a larger work bag) out of the fabric. Pin and sew a small 1.5 cm hem around each piece.

2. Transfer the embroidery design onto the white silk and work the stitches as per the design drawing.

3. Fold over a 3 cm casing along the top edge of each piece, so that the seam is on the inside of the piece. Iron and pin into place before stitching along the folded edge.

4. Pin the three sides together, with right sides together. Sew around the three sides, ending at the casing on each side. Do not sew over the casing ends.

5. Turn the work bag the right way out and iron the seams neatly.

6. Thread the ribbon through the casing and sew the ends of the ribbon together. Hide the ribbon end in the casing. There should be a gap at either end of the casing to allow the ribbon to form two handles.

Paper flowers

Novels *Persuasion, Mansfield Park, Pride and Prejudice, Northanger Abbey and Emma*

Regency Christmas celebrations charted a course between the abolitionist Puritans and the commercialised Victorians. As part of the English Revolution, Oliver Cromwell's parliament had banned Christmas, including the public holiday, as an attempt to reclaim the Christian purity of the event. Later, Queen Victoria and Prince Albert's love of Christmas and German traditions helped make it a populist affair. For example, while the Christmas tree was known in Britain during the Regency it had not yet become widespread. Its beautiful glass and wooden decorations were popular in the German states and much loved by Queen Victoria.

Christmas Day did not become a public holiday until well after the end of the Regency, meaning that towns and cities were still bustling with shops open on Christmas Day. Despite this lack of a public holiday, the mid-term break for schools and universities meant that Christmas was often a time to visit family and friends. Catherine's brother, James Morland visits the Thorpe family in *Northanger Abbey* over Christmas, while John and Isabella Knightley visit the Woodhouses in *Emma*. Writing to Mr and Mrs Gardiner after her engagement to Darcy is announced, Elizabeth Bennet provides them with an alternative Christmas venue from her parents' home and liberally invites them to Pemberley.

'*You are all to come to Pemberley at Christmas*'.
Pride and Prejudice

The holidays, with an influx of family and friends home for Christmas, were an ideal opportunity for balls and dinners, such as Mr and Mrs Weston's dinner in *Emma*. When Caroline Bingley writes to Jane Bennet, in *Pride and Prejudice*, to inform her of their departure to London, she alludes to such gaieties of the season.

'*I sincerely hope that your Christmas in Hertfordshire may abound in the gaieties which that season generally brings, and that your beaux will be so numerous as to prevent your feeling the loss of the three, of whom, we shall deprive you*'.
Pride and Prejudice

Christian responsibility, though, also firmly underpinned Christmas gift giving and celebrations. A typical Christmas Day involved church attendance, before a meal with family followed by readings and some suitable, fun games. Gift giving between family members was not a high priority. Depending on the tradition followed, small useful gifts may be given on St Nicholas' Day, 6 December, or on the twelfth night of Christmas, 6 January. However, much needed gifts of food or clothing to the poor of the Parish, servants and tenants were an important part of Christmas, taking place on Boxing Day.

In the depths of silver-white winters, greenery such as laurel, holly or mistletoe was used to decorate the house, twisted into wreaths for doors or bordering a cornice with paper rosettes. The availability of coloured paper also presented opportunities for decoration. In *Persuasion*, the Musgroves' children are home at Christmas cutting up silk and gold paper. In the days before Christmas trees became widely popular and needed decoration, it is likely the girls were making bon-bon boxes or cornucopias to be filled with sweets.

Immediately surrounding Mrs Musgrove were the little Harvilles, whom she was sedulously guarding from the tyranny of the two children from the Cottage, expressly arrived to amuse them. On one side was a table occupied by some chattering girls, cutting up silk and gold paper; and on the other were tressels and trays, bending under the weight

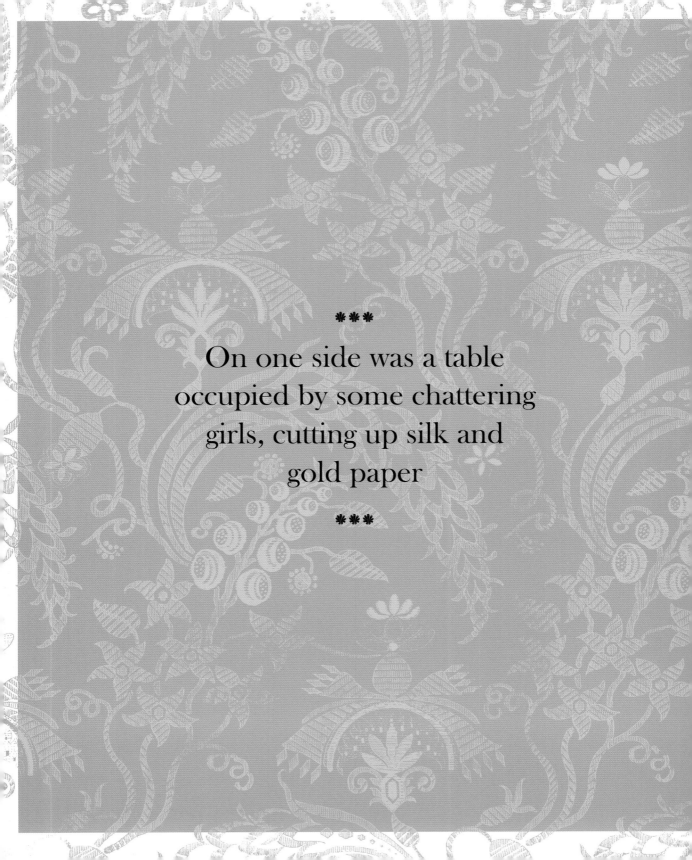

✳✳✳

On one side was a table
occupied by some chattering
girls, cutting up silk and
gold paper

✳✳✳

of brawn and cold pies, where riotous boys were holding high revel; the whole completed by a roaring Christmas fire, which seemed determined to be heard, in spite of all the noise of the others...It was a fine family—piece.

Persuasion

Likewise in *Mansfield Park*, the young Miss Bertrams, on Fanny Price's arrival, resort to making artificial flowers as a holiday pastime.

The holiday allowed to the Miss Bertrams the next day on purpose to afford leisure for getting acquainted with, and entertaining their young cousin, produced little union. They could not but hold her cheap on finding that she had but two sashes, and had never learnt French; and when they perceived her to be little struck with the duet they were so good as to play, they could do no more than make her a generous present of some of their least valued toys, and leave her to herself, while they adjourned to whatever might be the favourite holiday sport of the moment, making artificial flowers or wasting gold paper.

Mansfield Park

❋ ❋ ❋

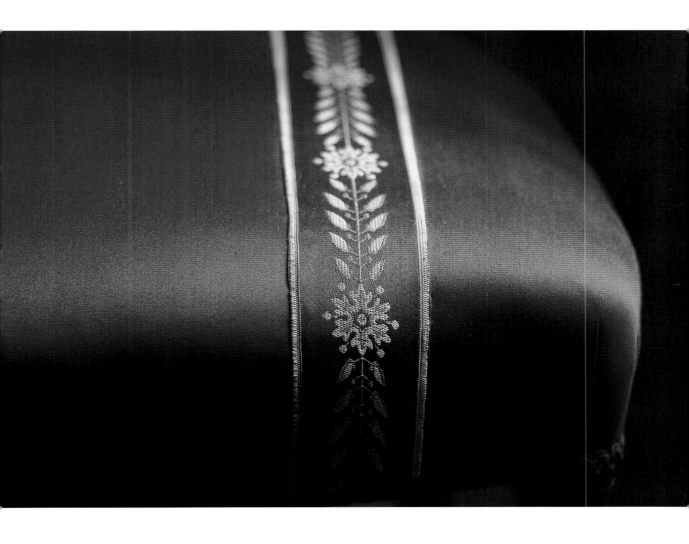

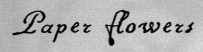

Paper flowers

MATERIALS

* 1 x sheet of rice or silk paper or firm tissue paper (1 sheet approximately 40 x 80 cm of rice paper will make five flowers)
* 2 m x 3 mm matching ribbon
* Sewing thread
* White glue
* Petal templates

TOOLS

* Sharp pointed scissors
* Drying space
* 4H Pencil
* Paint brush

diagram 1

Petal templates
Actual size

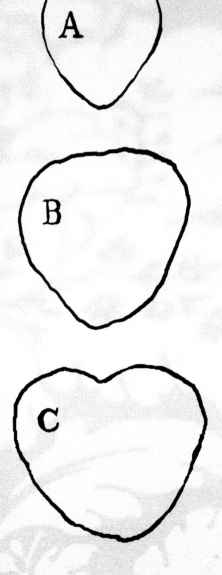

INSTRUCTIONS

1. Trace and cut out the petal templates onto the flower paper in the following quantities: 6 x Petal A, 4 x Petal B and 4 x Petal C.

2. Using the flower paper, make a small 1 cm ball of paper by placing a spot of glue in the middle of a square of paper and rolling into a ball. The ball becomes the flower base.

3. Brush glue onto the base of one Petal A and press firmly to the side of the ball of paper. Glue all the remaining Petal As around the ball.

4. Allow the petals to dry. Cut a 10 x 1 cm strip of flower paper and brush glue lightly onto the strip. Firmly wind the strip around the base of the petals (Diagram 1).

5. Glue the four Petal Bs around the base ensuring the petals are spaced around the ball evenly.

6. Glue the four Petal Cs around the base at alternate intervals to the Petal Bs.

7. Allow the petals to dry. Cut a second 10 x 1 cm strip of flower paper and brush glue lightly onto the strip. Firmly wind the strip around the base of the petals and leave to dry. This makes a stem.

Technique Knitting
& Netting
Level Intermediate/
Advanced

Purses

Novels *Pride and Prejudice, Persuasion,*
Northanger Abbey, Mansfield Park

❋ ❋ ❋

Jane Austen's novels are set in a world where money and how the family
earns it defines their place in the social order. Working for money was seen
as rather unfortunate, something that only those further down the social
ladder were forced to do out of necessity. Income, and ideally substantial
income derived from landed estates and investments in government
bonds, was necessary to claim one's place in the aristocracy and gentry
of the Regency Era. Large estates such as Mr Darcy's Pemberley and
Mr Knightley's Donwell Abbey supported entire districts through direct
employment of agricultural workers, or through tenant farming. Careful

stewardship of their landed estates ensured a substantial income for the family and safekeeping of the property for descendants. Earning a decent income through trade or other commercial and professional pursuits secured a place in the middle classes, and the disdain of the Emma Woodhouses' of the time.

This social order, and Jane Austen's challenge to it, underpins many of her novels—from Jane and Elizabeth Bennet marrying significantly above their income class, to Anne Elliot choosing a newly-wealthy naval captain, contrary to family expectations. Jane Austen also knew her family's place in the order when she described a social visit in 1807.

'I suppose they must be acting by the orders of Mr Lance of Netherton in this civility, as there seems no other reason for their coming near us. They will not come often, I dare say. They live in a handsome style and are rich, and she seemed to like to be rich, and we gave her to understand that we were far from being so; she will soon feel therefore that we are not worth her acquaintance.'

The acquisition of consumer goods, furniture, dresses, quantity of servants, carriages and horses, town houses and visits to London, were symbols of place within the social order. By the Regency Era, most substantial towns and the cities boasted banks, coffee houses and speciality stores such as the linen draper—which sold all sorts of fabric and haberdashery—tailors, milliners, shoe makers and toy shops. Circulating libraries held books, newspapers and, particularly in rural areas, also stocked other useful items like stockings and ribbons. Added to this was a layer of enterprising individuals such as travelling salesmen and mantua-makers (dress makers) who operated from their own homes.

Coins and paper money were in wide circulation by the Regency period, with paper notes introduced in the late 1600s by the Bank of England. Smaller rural banks also printed their own paper money. Small purses were used by both men and women to hold their currency and were popular gifts amongst family members. Purses were kept by women in their reticule (handbag) and by men in their pockets and were often small enough that they could be grasped in the hand.

Purses were netted or knitted. Netting was a popular pastime for both men and women. Women who netted cloaks and purses picked up the skill of making fishing or hunting nets, a male domestic occupation. Captain Harville in *Persuasion* uses his spare time to make fishing nets.

Captain Harville was no reader…his lameness prevented him from taking much exercise, but a mind of usefulness and ingenuity seemed to furnish him with constant employment within. He drew, he varnished, he carpentered, he glued, he made toys for the children, he fashioned new netting needles and pins with improvements, and if everything else was done, sat down to his large fishing net at one corner of the room.

Persuasion

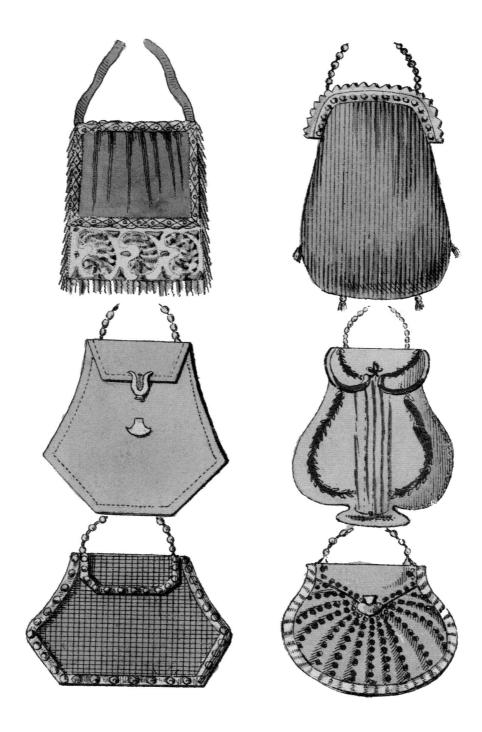

Netting purses was particularly popular, as Bingley comments below, with the body of the purse made of netting or this net could be laid over another fabric for contrast.

'All young ladies accomplished! My dear Charles, what do you mean?'
'Yes all of them I think. They all paint tables, cover screens and net purses. I scarcely know anyone who can not do all this, and I am sure I never heard a young lady spoken of for the first time, without being informed that she was very accomplished'.

Pride and Prejudice

Netting was such a common activity that netting boxes were often gifts; Fanny was the recipient of many a box in *Mansfield Park*. The box would hold fine netting cotton, a netting needle to hold the thread, a clamp to hold the net to a table and a gauge for making the spaces even.

Knitting did not enjoy such wide popularity during the Regency Era; it was not a fancy work for company but rather a useful craft, usually employed by older women and by poorer people who knitted stockings for sale. However, many examples of knitted purses remain from the era and knitted items were purchased, via Nurse Rooke, from the younger Mrs Smith in *Persuasion*.

The miser's purse, while used by both men and women, was a gift often made by women for male relatives in both knitted and netted materials. Two silver or gold rings were placed at each end of the opening in the miser's purse to keep the coins in. The miser's purse was often decorated with beading, tassels or pearl and shell ornaments secured at the ends. The small coin purse, used by women, was often decorated with beads or knitted patterns such as flowers. Metal clasps or drawstrings were used to close the small coin purse. Both patterns for purses can be worked in knitted or netted materials.

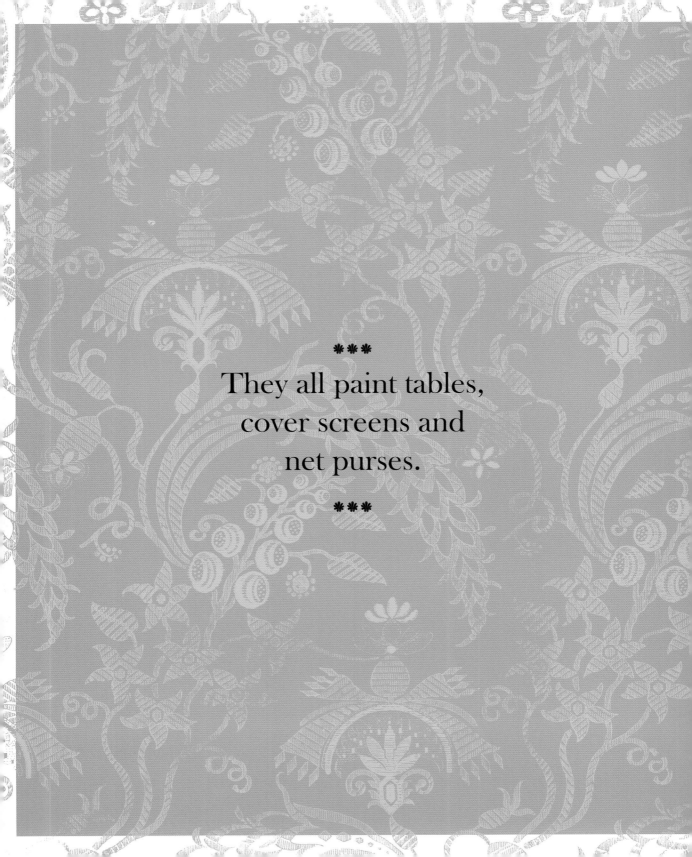

***

They all paint tables,
cover screens and
net purses.

***

Knitted miser's purse

Finished size: 36 cm with tassels

MATERIALS

* Knitting and Crochet 100% Cotton
  (4-ply equivalent)—can be worked with
  one strand or double strand of yarn
* Two silver dress rings (small to medium size)
* Matching silver beads

TOOLS

* Matching knitting needles
  (eg 3.25 mm for 4-ply equivalent)
* Scissors
* Wool needle

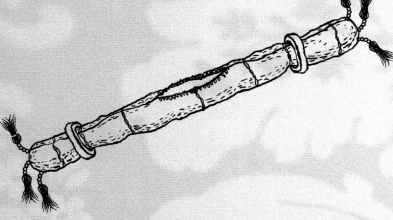

INSTRUCTIONS

1. Cast on 16 stitches, stocking stitch for 5 rows (K, P, K, P, K) then commence pattern below:

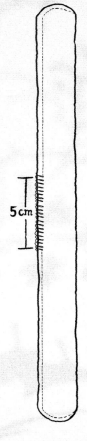

Row

1	Knit two together along row end with 8 stitches	**10**	Knit
2	Knit into the front and back of each stitch — by the end of this row should now have 16 stitches again	**11**	Purl
		12	Knit
		13	Purl
		14	Knit
3	Purl	**15**	Knit two together along row end with 8 stitches
4	Knit		
5	Purl		
6	Knit	**16**	Knit into the front and back of each stitch — by the end of this row should now have 16 stitches again
7	Purl		
8	Knit		
9	Purl		

2. Repeat Rows 3 to 16 until the pattern is repeated 7 times, finishing on row 16. To finish the piece, stocking stich for 5 rows (K, P, K, P, K) and cast off.

3. Finished piece is now 30 cm. Turn right sides together and, using a wool needle threaded with the cotton, sew the tube together, leaving a 5 cm open gap in the middle.

4. Sew the ends together; gather them into a rounded edge.

5. Hem the open gap in the middle with a row of stitches to firm the edge (Diagram 1).

6. Turn right way out, poking out ends. Slip the two rings on to sit in the centre, either side of the opening. The rings hold the coins in the purse.

7. Decorate the end of the purse with beads and tassels.

5 cm

Diagram 1

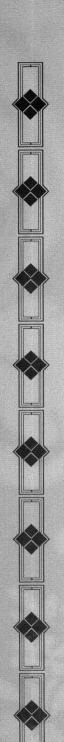

Netted coin purse

The netted fabric can be backed with another plain fabric such as silk to give a contrasting colour.

Finished size: 7 x 8 cm

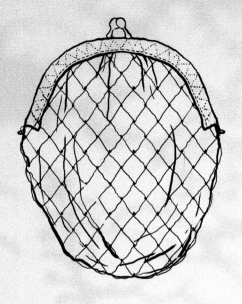

MATERIALS

* Thin crochet cotton (4-ply equivalent) or a DMC Cotton Perle Size 5
* 20 x 20 cm square of silk or cotton
* Silver metal purse frame or clasp (6 cm wide) or drawstring
* Matching thread

TOOLS

* Netting needle
* Gauge of desired size of net holes (8 mm holes used in purse pictured)
* Sewing needles
* Scissors

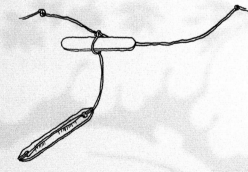

diagram 1

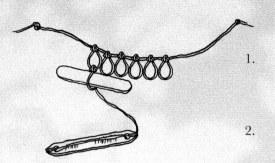

diagram 2

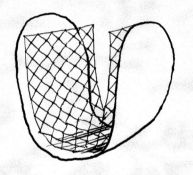

diagram 3

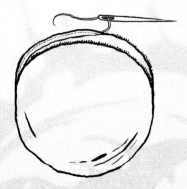

diagram 4

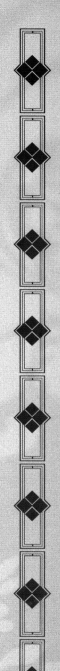

INSTRUCTIONS

1.   To make diamond shaped netting fabric for the coin purse, work a 12 x 24 cm rectangle as follows (or 10 x 30 cm for the miser's purse).

2.   Take a long thread of cotton and make a large loop with it, pin each end of the loop to a work mat or table.

3.   Wrap the cotton onto the netting needle. Tie one end to the long thread of cotton made at step 2.

4.   Hold the gauge against the long thread of cotton and wrap the thread from the netting needle around the gauge once. Make a knot against the gauge to form the first loop (Diagram 1). Continue along the row making a series of even sized loops against the gauge.

5.   To make a second row of loops (Diagram 2), turn the piece of netting so that the right side where the thread finished in step three now becomes the left side or beginning edge. Work each row from left to right.

6.   To work the second row, hold the gauge underneath the first loop from the first row and make another loop knotting off against the gauge. Keeping this new loop on the gauge, pick up the second loop from the first row and make another

97
Purses

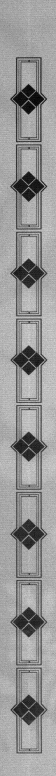

loop knotting off against the gauge. Keeping all the new loops made in the second row, continue down the row until two rows of loops have been made.

7. Turn the finished second row to work from left to right again. Repeat for each consecutive row until work measures desired length.

8. For a netted miser's purse make up the netted fabric following steps 2 to 6 in the knitted miser's purse instructions above.

9. For the coin purse, cut two oval shapes 10 cm long by 8 cm high out of the silk.

10. Fold the netted piece in half. Place the netting in the middle of the two oval pieces of silk (Diagram 3) and pin all four layers together to hold in place. Sew around the base of the oval shape, securing all four layers. Leave the top half of the oval open.

11. Turn the top raw edge over and sew a small hem securing the netting to the silk on each side of the purse opening (Diagram 4).

12. Turn the piece the right way out. Stitch the raw edge into the purse frame if it has holes. Alternatively, if using a purse frame that crimps shut, carefully place the top edge of the oval shape into the frame before crimping firmly.

Huswife

Novels *Emma, Sense and Sensibility*

❃ ❃ ❃

Sewing, and needlework, was often referred to as women's 'work' during the Regency Era, and all women were expected to sew. Women spent most of their time on plain sewing, making clothes for themselves or family members and making or mending linen and other household items. Even if wealthy women had a dressmaker, they would still make clothes for poor families, do their own alterations and make or decorate some clothes, such as shirts for the men of their family or as gifts.

Wealthy women were also expected to perfect their skill in fancy work, such as embroidery and carpet work (canvas work). Unlike plain

sewing, completed in the morning before visitors came, fancy work was performed in the company of visitors and guests, often as a sign of the skill and leisure time enjoyed by the women of the family.

The huswife was a small fabric case with pockets to hold all those tools for sewing and needlework needed quickly and often—scissors, needles, tape measure, thread, pins and pin cushion. The huswife was an indispensable tool for all women who spent a large part of the day on their work. The ordinariness of the huswife is seen in *Emma* when Miss Bates misplaces a letter from Jane Fairfax, that she later reads to Emma, by placing her huswife on it.

'Thank you. You are so kind!' replied the happily deceived aunt, while eagerly hunting for the letter. 'Oh here it is. I was sure it could not be far off, but I had put my huswife upon it, you see, and without being aware, and so it was quite hid'

Emma

Huswives were also given as gifts. At the age of 17, Jane Austen made a huswife with a matching bag for a family friend and neighbour, Mary Lloyd, when she left the district. In *Sense and Sensibility* the gift of a huswife each to Miss (Anne) Steele and her sister Lucy Steele by Fanny Dashwood is offered as both evidence of Fanny's disregard for her husband's half-sisters (Elinor and Marianne) and the mercenary nature of Miss Steele.

'And your brother and sister were not very kind! however, I shan't say anything against them to you; and to be sure they did send us home in their own chariot, which was more than I looked for. And for my part, I was all in a fright for fear your sister should ask us for the huswifes she had given us a day or two before, but, however, nothing was said about them, and I took care to keep mine out of sight'.

Miss Anne Steele to Miss Elinor Dashwood, *Sense and Sensibility*

Linen, cotton, wool and muslin were the most common types of fabrics available during the Regency Era. Huswives from that time were made from a range of fabrics and were many different shapes and sizes, from cylinders and rolled cases to a three-fold pocket. The instructions on page 111 are for a modest sized two-fold pocket suitable for most modern sewing tools. The sprigged pattern of small leaves and flowers used for our example was a popular Regency fabric pattern.

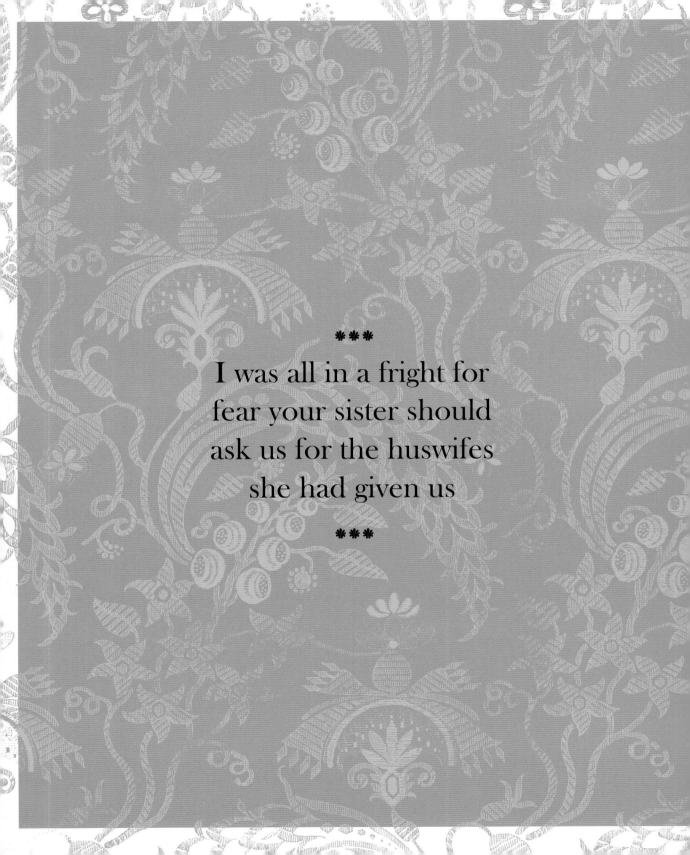

***

I was all in a fright for
fear your sister should
ask us for the huswifes
she had given us

***

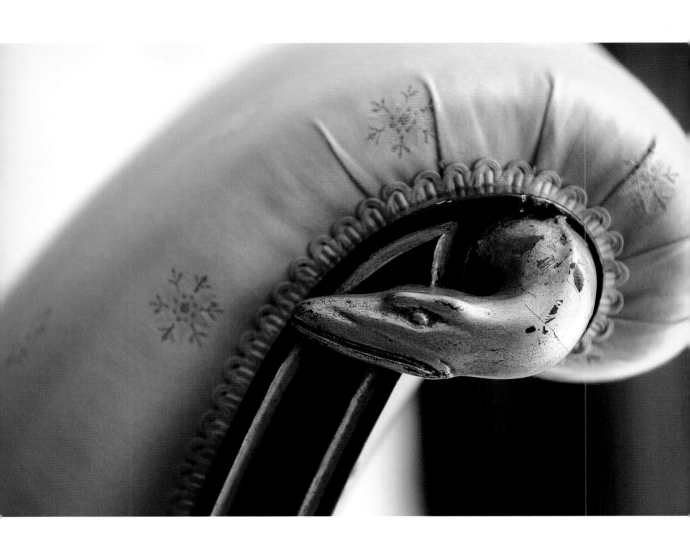

huswife

Finished size: 20 x 32 cm

MATERIALS

* 26 x 36 cm piece of decorative stiff fabric for outside of case (e.g. a firm cotton)
* 60 x 60 cm piece of plain firm lining fabric (also used for pockets)
* 40 x 40 cm piece of thin quilt wadding (e.g. wool wadding)
* 1 m of ribbon (for tying huswife together, 1 cm ribbon width)
* 50 cm of ribbon (for tying scissors in place)
* 1 Reel of sewing thread in matching colour

TOOLS

* Fabric scissors
* Tape measure
* Pins
* Sewing machine (can also be made by hand)
* Pencil

diagram 1

INSTRUCTIONS

1. If the decorative fabric for the outside of case is not 26 x 36 cm, measure and cut out this rectangle.

2. Measure, mark and cut out a rectangle 26 x 36 cm from the lining fabric.

3. Measure, mark and cut out a rectangle 26 x 36 cm from the thin wadding. You should now have three pieces which each measure 26 x 36 cm — decorative fabric, lining fabric and thin wadding.

4. Measure, mark and cut out a rectangle 24 x 15 cm from the lining fabric. This becomes the large internal pocket.

5. Measure, mark and cut out a rectangle 13 x 11 cm from the lining fabric. This becomes the small internal pocket.

6. Quilt the decorative fabric to the rectangle of thin wadding using diagonal straight lines 3 cm apart from each other in matching thread (Diagram 1). You may wish to mark out the diagonal lines 3 cm apart before sewing down each line. Set aside this quilted piece when finished.

7. Take the large pocket piece cut from the lining fabric. Fold over a 1.5 cm hem and iron into place. Sew top hem first, then pin the pocket into place on the lining. Sew the two pieces together around the three sides, keeping the hem under. Leave top edge open to form a pocket.

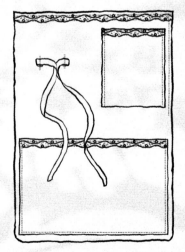

diagram 2

8. Take the small pocket piece cut from the lining fabric and repeat step seven to form a small pocket.

9. Cut the 50 cm piece of ribbon into half, giving you two pieces 25 cm long. Sew one piece of ribbon onto lining then sew other piece of ribbon 3 cm away from first piece in a horizontal line. This becomes your scissor tie (Diagram 2).

10. Place lining piece and decorative external quilted piece right sides together, so the pockets and ribbon are on the inside. Pin together leaving a 12 cm gap in the top right hand corner. Sew around this rectangle, except for this gap.

11. Turn the rectangle the right way out so that the decorative fabric is on one side and the pockets and ribbon facing out on the other side. Poke out the rectangle so it is neat and the corners are to your liking. Pin the 12 cm gap at the top right hand corner together. Iron around whole rectangle. Then sew the 12 cm gap together. Iron finished seams.

12. Take 1 m of ribbon and sew to middle edge on the outside of huswife where you want it to act as a tie.

Carpetwork

Novels *Emma, Mansfield Park, Pride and Prejudice, Sense and Sensibility*

❈ ❈ ❈

A distinctive feature of the Georgian and Regency Eras was the beauty of the architecture and interior design. With increased wealth filtering through the social order, new manufacturing techniques and the widespread availability of consumer goods, it was the first time that a large number of people could afford to take an interest in design. The gentry, the growing middle classes and families with wealth newly acquired through commerce or naval prizes, were keen to emulate the leaders of fashion. Emulation took many forms, from the purchase of goods for the home, to visits to the grand estates of Britain. In *Pride and Prejudice* the frequency of such visits is shown by Elizabeth's thoughts upon her tour with Mr and Mrs Gardiner.

Elizabeth was distressed. She felt that she had no business at Pemberley, and was obliged to assume a disinclination for seeing it. She must own that she was tired of great houses; after going to so many, she really had no pleasure in fine carpets or satin curtains. Mrs Gardiner abused her stupidity. 'If it were merely a fine house richly furnished,' said she, 'I should not care about it myself; but the grounds are delightful. They have some of the finest woods in the country'.

Pride and Prejudice

The Prince Regent, the Prince of Wales, lead the enthusiastic interest in architecture and interior design through constant remodelling of his primary residence, Carlton House in London. Key design influences of the period were implemented in the house, from the Neo-classical exterior, to the vibrant red drawing room and the Gothic dining room. The house was also liberally furnished with ornaments and furniture inspired by Chinoiserie, or Chinese inspired patterns and design, and the Gothic. Jane Austen visited the Prince Regent's Librarian, Reverend James Stanier Clarke, at Carlton House in 1815. During his regency and later reign as King George IV, the Prince Regent also had The Royal Pavilion in Brighton remodelled by John Nash (1815–1823). The pavilion's exterior illustrates the Indian and Moorish styles, which along with Egyptian, were popular in the later part of the Regency Era, while the interiors exhibited the Gothic as well as Chinese and Indian inspired design.

There were many influences on both architecture and interior design, with many families borrowing a slice of one or more influences to modernise their homes. The excavation of Pompeii in 1748 and the tradition of the Grand Tour among wealthy young gentleman from Britain, through France to the Italian States, fostered an interest in the classical, ordered lines of ancient antiquity, firstly ancient Rome and then ancient Greece. This style became known as Neo-classicism, with many villas, cottages and grand estates being rebuilt entirely in this style or with certain features such as columns added.

Another of the great influences on design was the antithesis of Neo-classicism and an aspect of Romanticism, the Medieval and the Gothic with its turrets, gargoyles, arches, confusion and irregular lines. Commonly associated with great cathedrals and abbeys built during the medieval period, this style was adapted to residences by adding gothic arches and windows or deliberately creating irregular lines through extensions and rooms without a thought to symmetry.

The detail of interiors became increasingly important due to greater visibility inside the house and the wide availability of consumer goods, such as fabrics, furniture and wallpaper. The popularity of the large six-panel by six-panel windows allowed more light into rooms. An interior then became the sum of each carefully chosen piece, from the banister rails, architraves, window sashes, paint, hung wallpapers, and soft furnishings to the Wedgewood porcelain sets, such as the set that the Austens purchased in June 1811, delivered to their home at Chawton.

***

She really had no
pleasure in fine carpets
or satin curtains

***

The colour of the interiors changed throughout the period so that any home may have exhibited the early Georgian colours of stone, pale and medium greens, blues including sky and slate blues, soft greys and pinks and the later bold colours such as rich reds and vivid yellows.

With such an interest in design, it is not surprising that women turned their needlework and other creative pursuits to the decoration of the interiors of their home. Along with the painting of tables and the construction of fire screens and footstools, women also created needleworked pieces of carpetwork. Now known as canvas work, this was coloured wool worked on a firm grid canvas used to make soft furnishings such as bed valances, rugs and pillows.

Carpetwork may have been largely been associated with older women, as Lady Bertram in *Mansfield Park* and Mrs Jennings and Mrs Fanny Dashwood in *Sense and Sensibility* undertake carpetwork. Emma clearly associates carpetwork with an occupation for older women, when she tells Harriet that she has little intention of marrying and lists the possible pastimes for an unmarried woman.

'...And I do not perceive why I should be more in want of employment at forty or fifty than one and twenty. Woman's usual occupations of eye, and hand, and mind, will be as open to me then as they are now, or with no important variation. If I draw less, I shall read more, if I give up music, I shall take up carpet work'.

Emma

Chinoiserie carpetwork pillow

MATERIALS

* 9 x DMC Tapestry wool medium green No: 7326
* 20 x DMC Tapestry wool light green No: 7322
* 3 x DMC Tapestry wool light pink No: 7223
* 3 x DMC Tapestry wool medium pink No: 7226
* 45 x 33 cm tapestry canvas (10 count)
* 1 x 1 m plain firm backing fabric
* Sewing thread
* 30 x 30 cm cushion insert

TOOLS

* Tapestry or wool needle
  (firm with a blunt end)
* Scissors
* Washable marking pen or pencil
* Tapestry frame

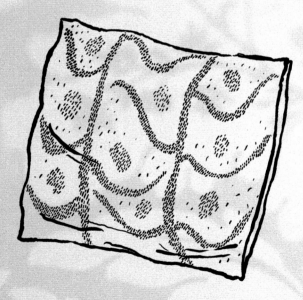

INSTRUCTIONS

1. Attach canvas to tapestry frame using the manufacturer's instructions for the frame.

2. Photocopy the pattern by 200% for the pictured cushion with a 30 x 30 cm cushion insert.

3. Transfer design onto the canvas with a transfer pen.

4. Using half cross stitch fill in the transferred canvas design using the colours in the pattern indicated.

5. When complete remove from frame, iron and trim to a 35 cm square.

6. The back of the cushion cover is made from two overlapping fabric pieces. A pocket is formed, into which a cushion can be inserted.

7. Cut two pieces of fabric for the back — each piece measures 35 x 45 cm, allowing a 5 cm seam allowance. Hem neatly around each piece.

8. Take one of the back pieces and place it face down on the front of the canvas work. Pin it so that three edges of the back piece are lined up with three edges of the canvas work. Sew these edges together.

9. Leave the fourth edge of the back piece unattached.

10. Take the other back piece and repeat steps 8–9 to form a pocket at the opposite end of canvas work. These two pockets should overlap by 10 cm in the middle of the back (Diagram 1).

11. Turn the cushion cover the right way out. Poke out the corners and put the cushion insert inside.

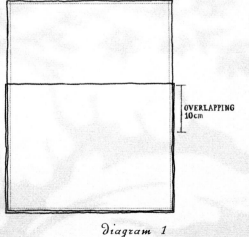

OVERLAPPING
10 cm

Diagram 1

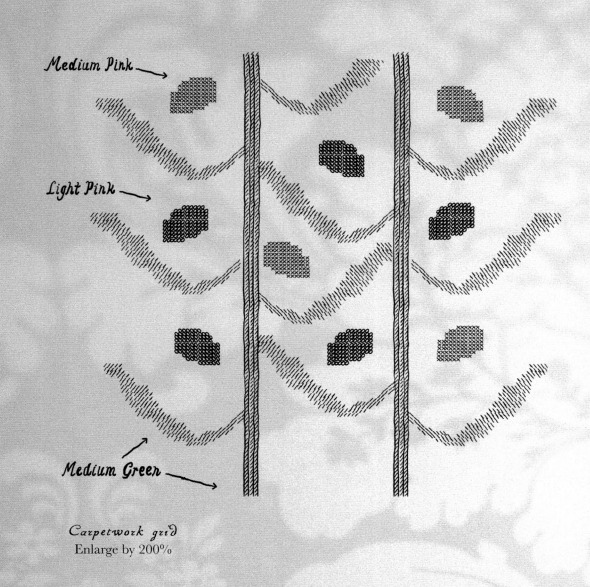

Medium Pink

Light Pink

Medium Green

Carpetwork grid
Enlarge by 200%

Muff and Tippet

Novels *Emma*, *Northanger Abbey*, *Sense and Sensibility*

❋ ❋ ❋

Regency Era women's fashion was defined by classical lines, beautiful fabrics and exquisite, if often simple, embellishments. The beginning of the era opened with the high-waisted, narrow-bodiced dresses inspired by ancient Rome and Greece and it closed with some modification such as fuller sleeves, lower waistlines and more rounded skirts with greater decoration. Of course fashion was inevitably tempered by the practical realities of daily life and the weather.

Women of varying degrees of wealth and leisure dressed for each occasion, with up to three or four dress changes a day. The morning dress was a practical garment, usually of a dark colour and made from heavy fabric such as a stiff cotton or wool to protect the dress from any necessary chores. A full-length apron was worn over the dress to protect it from dirt or damage while, for example, washing the families' clothes, which in many families involved not only the servants but the women of the household as well. A walking dress, specifically for outdoor wear could be the same dress or another dress suitable for outdoors with a slightly raised hem to keep it out of the mud, long sleeved and usually a dark colour.

Evening wear, for young women in particular, was the opportunity to display the latest fashions. White muslin was the first choice for evening occasions, though silks, satins and velvets remained popular. White layers of muslin were often decorated with white or coloured embroidery or coloured sashes. A dress of colour was also worn under one or two layers of white muslin, for example a yellow cotton dress under a layer of muslin, with descending rows of matching yellow ribbon below the knee stitched onto the muslin.

Writing to Cassandra in 1801, Jane Austen illustrates the distinction between dresses in fabric and colour appropriate to the occasion.

'I shall want two new coloured gowns for the summer, for my pink one will not do more than clear me from Steventon. I shall not trouble you, however, to get more than one of them, and that is to be a plain brown cambric muslin, for *morning wear, the other which is to be a very pretty yellow and white cloud, I mean to buy in Bath'.*

However a dress was just the top layer of a suite of clothes worn by women in all weather. Long-legged drawers were beginning to be worn during the Regency Era, usually made from cotton and reaching to below the knee. However, unlike hand-knitted or loom made stockings reaching to above the knee, they were not yet mandatory. A slip in linen or cotton was worn close to the skin, over which the stays or corset would be fitted and laced together. The slip provided both warmth and protection for finer fabrics from perspiration, while the stays ensured a straight figure, smoothing the stomach and supporting the bust. Depending on the weather, a further skirt of cotton or wool—a petticoat—was tied around the waist. The morning, walking or evening dress was worn over all of these layers.

The popularity of muslin made it difficult for the women of Britain to keep warm. It was common during the day, and for older women into the evenings as well, to wrap a triangle of lace or fabric, called a fichu, around the neck and tuck it into the low cut bodice of the dress. Alternatively a chemisette, like a waistcoat with a ruffled or high collar, was worn under the dress to poke up through the bodice to protect the chest and neck. A large shawl became a welcome accessory and was used both inside and outside.

Outdoor wear called for stronger and warmer fabrics which were used to make two pieces common to the era, the spencer and pelisse. A spencer was a long-sleeved half jacket which followed the high-waisted dresses and ended at the bodice line. A pelisse was a full-length coat,

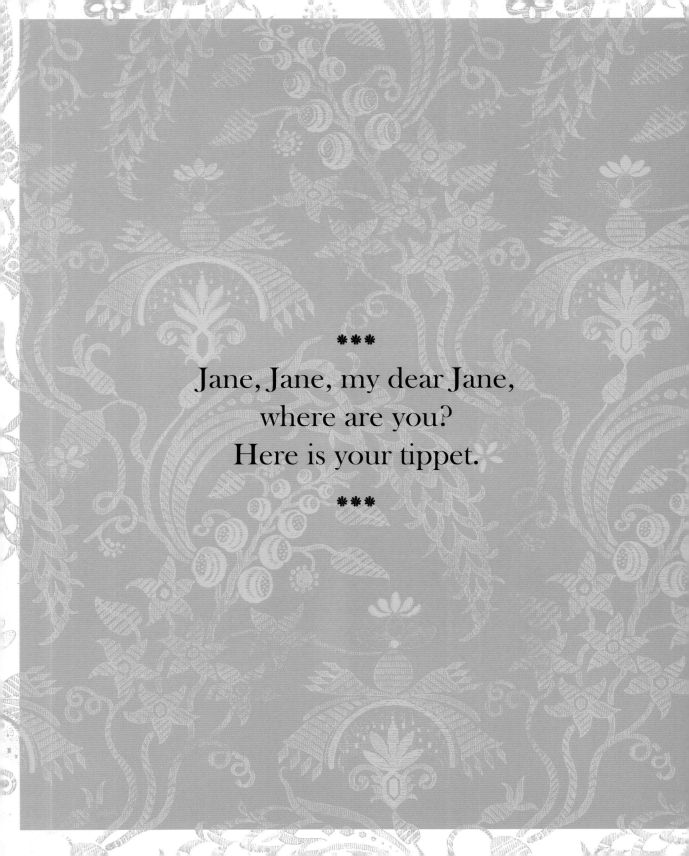

***

Jane, Jane, my dear Jane,
where are you?
Here is your tippet.

***

tailored to the style with a high waist. Gloves and a bonnet or hat were also always worn, whatever the weather.

In winter a muff and tippet were also common additions to an oufit. During the Regency Era muffs were large, luxurious accessories in which to keep gloved hands warm. On musing about the weather when visiting London, and in the hope that the colder weather would bring the men, including Willoughby, to town away from hunting in the country, Marianne Dashwood asks:

'Don't you find it colder than it was in the morning, Elinor? There seems to me a very decided difference. I can hardly keep my hands warm even in my muff. It was not so yesterday, I think.'

Sense and Sensibility

Commonly worn both indoors and outdoors, a tippet was a long loose scarf which sat around the neck, with the ends hung loosely, and unclipped, around the front. In *Emma*, as they move to supper during the Ball at the Crown, Miss Bates is anxious for Jane Fairfax to wear her tippet;

'Jane, Jane, my dear Jane, where are you? Here is your tippet. Mrs Weston begs you to put on your tippet. She says she is afraid there will be draughts in the passage, though *every thing has been done — One door nailed up — Quantities of matting — My dear Jane, indeed you must. Mr Churchill, oh! You are too obliging! How well you put it on!'*

Emma

In an era where the fur trade was a large part of international commerce and domestic hunting was common, the muff and tippet were made from fur. Jane Austen was given a much-admired gift of an ermine (a stoat, also called a weasel) tippet in 1814, meaning that it was probably mostly white in colour. Other common furs were rabbit and fox, with long soft fur of variable colours, and the beaver with thick dark brown fur. The reverse side of the fur tippet was sometimes lined with a simple fabric. Mrs Allen purchases a new muff and tippet in *Northanger Abbey*. The weight of the fur determined the price.

Inquiries and communications concerning brothers and sisters ...now passed between them, and continued with only one small digression on James's part...till they reached Pulteney-street, where he was welcomed with great kindness by Mr and Mrs Allen, invited by the former to dine with them, and summoned by the latter to guess the price and weigh the merits of a new muff and tippet.

Northanger Abbey

✷ ✷ ✷

Muff

Finished size : 40 x 50 cm tube

MATERIALS

* 45 x 55 cm of fake fur
* 45 x 55 cm of contrasting cotton fabric
* Sewing thread

TOOLS

* Tape measure
* Sewing machine
* Sewing needles
* Scissors

INSTRUCTIONS

1. Pin the contrasting cotton fabric to the fur, so that the right sides are together. Sew a 2.5 cm hem around the three sides of the rectangle.

2. Carefully trim the edge of the fur and cotton hem so that when turned out the seams are smooth and not too bulky.

3. Turn rectangle out the right way. Pin and tuck under the fourth side of the rectangle and sew neatly into place.

4. Pin two smaller lengths of the rectangle together (these sides should now measure about 40 cm) and hand sew into place to create a tube.

5. Optional: to show the contrasting fabric through the fur on the outside adjust step four to read:

   a. Cut a 45 x 6 cm strip of contrasting cotton, turn so the right sides are together and the strip is folded in half. Sew the ends of the strip leaving the long length open, turn right way out. Pin the two smaller lengths of the fur tube together, placing the strip of contrasting fabric in the middle, poking up through the fur right side up. Sew all three layers into place to create a tube, being careful to sew along the back of the contrasting fabric to hide the stitching underneath. When complete, smooth the cotton edge down to cover the stitches.

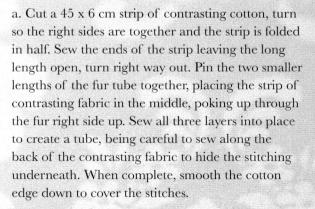

Tippet

Finished size: 80 cm long (from neck to end)

MATERIALS

* 50 cm x 1 m of fake fur
* 50 cm x 1 m of contrasting cotton fabric
* Sewing thread

TOOLS

* Tape measure
* Sewing machine
* Sewing needles

INSTRUCTIONS

1. Cut a piece of fur from the tippet pattern.

2. Cut a piece of cotton fabric from the tippet pattern.

3. Pin the cotton piece to the fur piece right sides together. Make sure it is pinned all the way around.

4. With the sewing machine or by hand, sew the two pieces together. It may be necessary to clip the curves round the neck line and at the ends to ease the fabric into place. Leave an opening at the base of the neck.

5. Turn the pieces out the right way, carefully poking out the scarf ends. Pin and sew under the opening at the base of the neck.

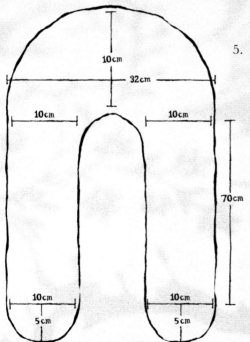

Pin cushion and Thread case

Novels *Persuasion, Pride and Prejudice, Emma*

❋ ❋ ❋

The Regency Era and Jane Austen's novels are associated in the modern mind with elegance and etiquette, beauty and romance, and wealth within a tight social order. However, sitting alongside the greatness that was late Georgian Britain, was also a society afflicted with poverty, and its companions—crime and illness.

As Britain took great strides in industry and agriculture, the towns and cities became a source of employment for people no longer needed in the fields. Jobs were found in manufacturing, such as the cotton factories, and on the docklands receiving the raw materials obtained through trade.

Work, though, did not translate into affluence, or in many cases even subsistence for the poor. Low wages and long hours were considered necessary to keep the poor industrious. Although a wealthy middle class was emerging Georgian society was still one in which people knew their place—and that was the one they were born into. Such exclusion from the wealth of the time also resulted in unprecedented levels of crime, particularly theft. Images of Georgian Britain not only include muslin and lace but also the miserable hulks sitting on the Thames, holding criminals awaiting transportation to the Americas and, later on, to Australia.

The French Revolution, with its violent overthrow of the monarchy and aristocracy, shocked the established order in Britain. Fearful of a similar event, the upper classes paid renewed attention to their traditional responsibility to alleviate the distress of the poor. The urban poor were caught outside the traditional welfare system based on rural landowners and relied on the benevolence, where it could be found, of their masters or the church.

It is the traditional welfare system that Jane Austen portrays in her novels. In rural areas, a man was judged a good landowner if he took great interest in the welfare of the workers on his estate and surrounding parish. In Jane Austen's novels the social responsibility of the wealthy classes is portrayed by Mr Darcy's and his father's concern for their estate and the poor, Emma Woodhouse's visit to Mrs and Miss Bates, and Anne Elliott's taking leave of 'every house in the parish' upon her departure to Uppercross.

In *Pride and Prejudice*, Elizabeth Bennet discovers Darcy's true character on her tour of Pemberley with Mrs Reynolds, the housekeeper.

Elizabeth almost stared at her. 'Can this be Mr. Darcy!' thought she.

'his father was an excellent man,' said Mrs. Gardiner.

'Yes, ma'am, that he was indeed; and his son will be just like him—just as affable to the poor.'

'he is the best landlord, and the best master,' said she, 'that ever lived.

Not like the wild young men now—a—days, who think of nothing but themselves.

There is not one of his tenants or servants but what will give him a good name.

Mrs Reynolds, Pemberley's housekeeper, to Elizabeth Bennet and Mr and Mrs Gardiner, *Pride and Prejudice*

A system of small, regular kindnesses underpinned assistance given to the poor within a parish, such as the bushel of apples that Mr Knightley gave to Miss Bates in *Emma*. It was also a sign of a wealthy woman's respectability if she devoted time and effort to the poor through making and mending clothes for them from the work basket and visiting the families of the parish, particularly in times of illness.

In *Persuasion* the young widow Mrs Smith clings to her position of genteel poverty and her claims to respectability by learning to knit items for sale from Nurse Rooke. She uses the proceeds of such sales to assist poorer families in the area.

Pin cushion and Thread case

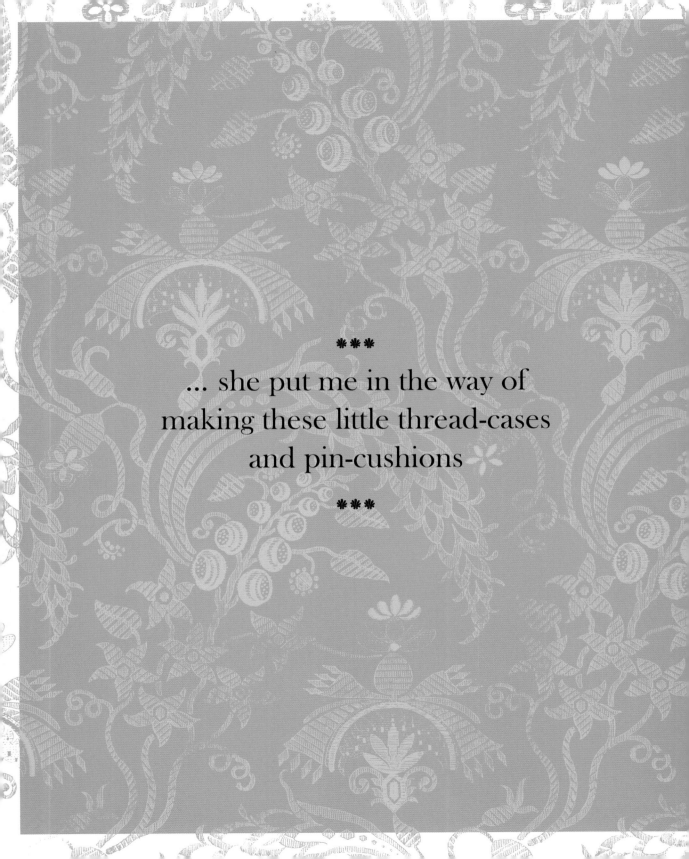

✳✳✳

... she put me in the way of
making these little thread-cases
and pin-cushions

✳✳✳

'And she', said Mrs Smith 'besides nursing me most admirably, has really proved an invaluable acquaintance. As soon as I could use my hands, she taught me to knit, which has been a great amusement, and she put me in the way of making these little thread—cases, pin—cushions and card—racks, which you always find me so busy about, and which supply with the means of doing a little good to one or two very poor families in this neighbourhood. She has a large acquaintance, of course professionally, among those who can afford to buy, and she disposes of my merchandise'.

Persuasion

Embroidery thread was sold loosely, either by yards or ounce, without spools or reels to contain it. Thread winders in bone or wood were needed to hold yards of thread. A thread case was then a clever item for sale as it held the thread winders and kept the required threads for a project together. Sewing pins were also more expensive than they are today so keeping pins secure was of greater importance. While Jane Austen describes Mrs Smith knitting her pin cushion and thread cases, these items were most commonly sewn from fabric remnants during this era. Sewn and embroidered pin cushions were often richly decorated and were given, along with the pins, as gifts.

❋ ❋ ❋

Pin cushion and Thread case

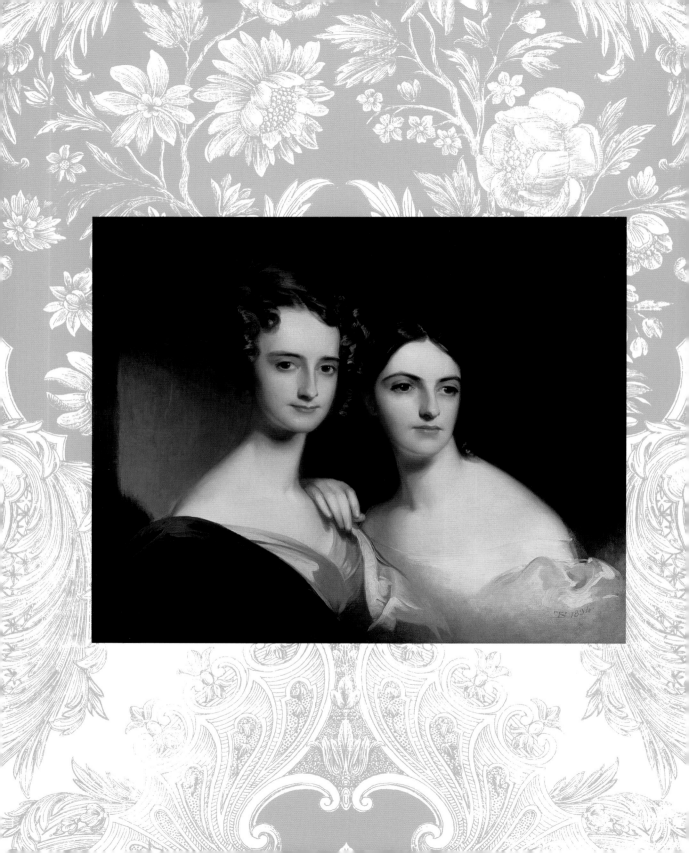

Thread case

Finished size: (open case): 25 x 8 cm
(to contain 6 to 9 thread winders)

MATERIALS

* 30 cm of fabric
* Silk thread (one skein for both projects)
* Contrasting trim such as ribbon or bias binding
* Small button (15 mm)

TOOLS

* Sewing needle or sewing machine
* Scissors
* Tape measure

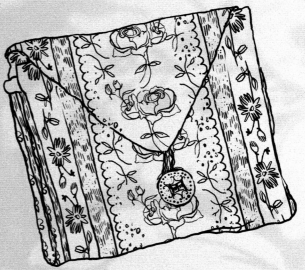

INSTRUCTIONS

1. Cut two pieces of fabric for the front and back panels of the thread case measuring 12 cm for the width, 23 cm for the length to the start of the triangle and an 8 x 8 cm triangle at one end.

2. Cut three pieces of fabric measuring 10 x 7 cm to become the pockets.

3. Hem each pocket around three sides, leaving the top edge raw.

4. Cut three lengths of the trim and stitch to this raw top edge on each pocket.

5. Sew the three pockets onto the right side of one of the panels of fabric. Leave a 1.5 cm space between each pocket.

6. With right sides together, stitch the two panels together — leaving the bottom edge open. Stitch the sides so that the pocket edges disappear into the side seams to create a smooth edge.

7. Turn the right way out and stitch neatly along the bottom edge.

8. Sew on the silk thread or ribbon, as a loop, to the top inside point of the triangle. This becomes a loop to hang the case by as well as to close it with the button. Decorate the pocket edges as desired.

9. On the outside of the thread case, sew the button in place where the loop will attach to hold the case together in a round.

151

Pin cushion and Thread case

Pin cushion

Finished size: 11 x 8 cm

MATERIALS

* 25 cm of fabric (two pieces of fabric 13 x 10 cm)
* Silk thread (one skein for both projects)
* Sewing thread
* Pearl beads
* Stuffing

TOOLS

* Sewing needles or sewing machine
* Scissors
* Tape measure

INSTRUCTIONS

1. With right sides together, sew a small seam around each side, leaving a 3 cm gap on the top left. Turn case the right way out

2. Make four tassels 3 cm in length and sew to three corners only. To make a tassel, wind the silk thread (all strands) four times around a 3 cm wide piece of card. Secure the loops with a separate strand before cutting the looped thread at the base of the card. Tie a firm thread around the top of the tassel, 0.5 cm from the top and trim the ends.

3. Sew a pearl bead at three corners and sew the tassels to the same three corners.

4. Stuff the pin cushion firmly. Sew up the 3 cm gap. Sew on the fourth tassel and bead, then sew a pearl bead in the middle of both sides of the cushion.

5. To make the twisted braid which edges the pin cushion, secure the end of the silk thread (all strands) to a table and twist the thread in the same direction several times until firm. Place a finger in the middle of the twisted thread and let the silk fold in on itself. Tie a knot at the end to keep the twist in place.

6. Couch the twisted braid around the seam joining the two fabric pieces. 'Couching' is to sew the braid to the fabric with small stitches in the same matching thread.

Pin cushion and Thread case

Transparency

Novels *Mansfield Park, Northanger Abbey, Sense and Sensibility*

'It is very true' said Marianne, 'that admiration of landscape scenery is become a mere jargon. Every body pretends to feel and tries to describe with the taste and elegance of him who first defined what picturesque beauty was.'
Sense and Sensibility

Romanticism was one of the major philosophical trends of the Regency Era, influencing architecture, literature and art in particular.

Its greatest influence was felt from the late 1700s to 1848, so it is not surprising that it is a recurrent theme throughout Jane Austen's novels. Romanticism was a style or a way of thinking rather than a clearly defined movement with set boundaries. It rejected the rationalism of the Enlightenment in favour of authentic emotion and response.

The Enlightenment, beginning in the late 1600s, brought science and reason to the natural, social and political fields. It challenged religion's expectation of faith without argument, with the view that reason and logic provided a more adequate explanation of the origins and meaning of life. The signature personalities of the era, Galileo and Newton, used mathematics and science to explain the natural world while Diderot's French *Encyclopédie* was one of the first attempts to organise and systemise knowledge.

To the Romantics such rationalism and organisation denied the human spirit, and like Marianne Dashwood in *Sense and Sensibility*, they believed in authentic emotions in the artistic endeavours as well as in personal behaviour. In architecture and art, British romantics reclaimed their heritage with a particular love of the medieval and gothic. Neo-classical buildings were considered inauthentic, not British and a derivative of the borrowed cultures of ancient Rome and Greece. While in literature, Mary Shelley's *Frankenstein: the Modern Prometheus* summarised what many romantics felt; that science and reason denied the reality of human existence—of family, relationships, love and God—with disastrous consequences. At a personal level, to hide feelings or emotions in the pursuit of politeness, is inauthentic and Elinor Dashwood is often left to smooth over the ruptures caused by Marianne's effusive displays of spontaneous emotion.

The Picturesque emerged amidst this resurgence of the human spirit, sharing with Romanticism an emphasis on emotional response. The Picturesque was particularly focused on an emotional appreciation of the beauty of nature. Such emotional appreciation was best developed through the experience of travel, initially to the European continent for those who could afford it, and often manifested in the creation and appreciation of art. The Picturesque encouraged both professional and amateur artists to view the natural surroundings, or landscape, as a picture in itself. Professional painters had previously focused on great historical or biblical events, with the landscape just a backdrop for human drama or associated with labouring peasants, unworthy of aristocratic contemplation. For the first time the landscape became a subject to be painted for its own sublime and beautiful qualities.

In *Northanger Abbey* Eleanor and Henry Tilney appreciate the landscape both for its beauty and its potential as a subject for drawing, leaving Catherine Morland floundering.

She knew nothing of drawing... she confessed and lamented her want of knowledge, declared that she would give anything in the world to be able to draw; and a lecture on the picturesque immediately followed, in which his instructions were so clear that she soon began to see beauty in everything admired by him. He talked of foregrounds, distances and second distances—side-screens and perspectives—lights and shades; and

***

His instructions were so clear
that she soon began to see
beauty in everything

***

Catherine was so hopeful a scholar that when they gained the top of Beechen Cliff, she voluntarily rejected the whole city of Bath as unworthy to make part of a landscape.
Northanger Abbey

Tourism at home grew as the Napoleonic wars made the Grand Tour of Europe impossible, fostering an interest in the Picturesque British countryside. Amateur artists, as holiday makers, now enthusiastically picked up their paints and followed in the footsteps of professional artists to seek an emotional experience in nature. In Britain this meant travelling to places considered to be of great beauty, the Lakes District in particular, or to Scotland, where Jane Austen's brother Henry travelled for a holiday in 1813 to enjoy the scenery.

The Picturesque was not yet the direct representation of the landscape that later artists like Constable practised—it demanded a bit of artistic licence. The idealised landscape in the Picturesque style required several elements, largely defined by Gilpin in the 1770s: a sense of proportion, a body of water, rugged mountains, an abbey, castle or ruin and a small group of three. If necessary the artist could easily add, modify or even borrow from the Continent if the reality of the British landscape was deficient.

An amusing discussion between Edward Ferrars and Marianne Dashwood in *Sense and Sensibility* highlights some of the 'standard' picturesque elements.

'You must not enquire too far, Marianne; remember I have no knowledge in the picturesque, and I shall offend you by my ignorance and want of taste if we come to particulars. I shall call hills steep, which ought to be bold; surfaces strange and uncouth, which ought to be irregular and rugged; and distant objects out of sight, which ought only to be indistinct through the soft medium of a hazy atmosphere. You must be satisfied with such admiration as I can honestly give... It exactly answers my idea of a fine country, because it unites beauty with utility'

Edward Ferrars to Marianne Dashwood, Sense and Sensibility

In *Mansfield Park* when Jane Austen places Fanny Price in her East Room she signals to the reader that the young Bertrams are practising amateur artists of the Picturesque with her reference to some of these required elements—the abbey, a cave in Italy and an English lake.

The room was most dear to her, and she would not have changed its furniture for the handsomest in the house, though what had been originally plain, had suffered all the ill-usage of children—and its greatest elegancies and ornaments were a faded footstool of Julia's work, too ill done for

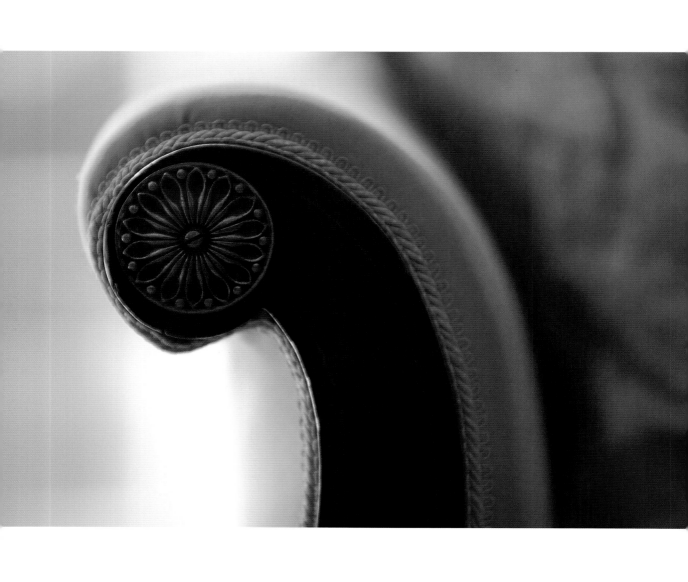

the drawing room, three transparencies, made in a rage for transparencies, for the three lower panes of one window, where Tintern Abbey held its station between a cave in Italy, and a moonlight lake in Cumberland, a collection of family profiles thought unworthy of anywhere else, over the mantle-piece.

Mansfield Park

The Bertrams, like many amateur artists of the period, were probably keen to turn their hand to the latest artistic style and the 'rage for transparencies'. The painting of transparent oils onto glass panes, allowed them to do so even if their artistic skill was lacking. Glass was becoming an increasingly popular building material and its increased availability opened up possibilities for both professional and amateur artists. Professional artists used transparencies to make copies of their works on canvas. The transparency was then back-lit so the professional artist could exhibit their work in public shows to large audiences. The artist would also often provide a lecture, allowing the leisured classes to further their understanding and appreciation of the Picturesque style. At the amateur level, wealthy women and girls sometimes preferred glass to a traditional canvas as a design could be traced onto the glass, then filled in with transparent oil paints. This transparency then created a modest stained glass effect when hung in a Georgian window. However as glass was not yet mass-produced it was still quite expensive, confining this pursuit to the wealthier classes, such as the residents of Mansfield Park.

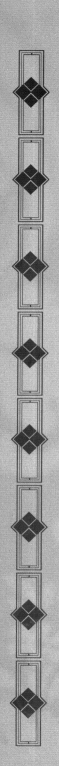

Transparency

MATERIALS

* 13 x 18 cm rectangle of glass
  (photo frames provide a suitable rectangle of glass)
* Black glass paint / liquid leading / leading tape
* 2 shades of pink glass paint
* 2 shades of green glass paint

TOOLS

* Very fine round paint brush
* Medium round paint brush
* Water
* Drawing template

Template
Enlarge by 150%

INSTRUCTIONS

1. Place the drawing template under the rectangle of glass. Use the fine tip of the round paint brush and your choice of outliner—black glass paint, liquid leading or leading tape to trace the outline of the oval, petunia and leaves onto the glass (Diagram 1). Allow the outline time to dry.

2. Fill the petunia in with the pink paints. The medium round brush can be used to give a light dab, producing a softer, hazed finish.

3. Colour the leaves in with the green paints.

4. Set the piece aside to dry for 6–8 hours before placing within a frame or window pane.

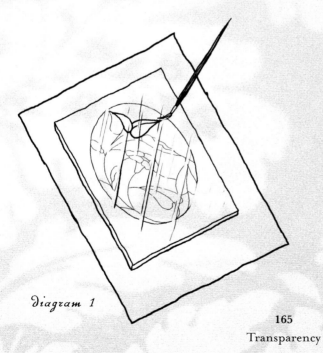

diagram 1

Bonnet

Novels *Sense and Sensibility, Pride and Prejudice,*
Mansfield Park, Northanger Abbey

❋ ❋ ❋

Bonnets, like many pieces of clothing in the Regency Era, were not only useful items but had an important role to play in signalling social and family status.

In line with the classical and natural forms of Regency dress, personal appearance was clean, simple and without the heavy makeup and adornment characteristic of earlier 18th century fashion. Hair was usually piled up upon the head with curls around the face and for special occasions decorated with flowers, ribbons or jewels. The face was to be as natural as possible with no makeup. The bonnet with a front brim, or the hat with a brim all the way around, were useful items in helping the face retain its natural state and protect it from the wind and sun. A line from *Mansfield Park* gives an indication of just how deep the brim of a bonnet could be in shading the face.

How her [Fanny] heart swelled with joy and gratitude as she passed the barriers of Portsmouth, and how Susan's face wore its broadest smiles, may be easily conceived. Sitting forwards, however, and screened by her bonnet, those smiles were unseen.

Mansfield Park

The style of a bonnet also signalled social and family status. In *Mansfield Park*, Tom Bertram recounts paying inappropriate attention to the younger sister of a friend who was not yet 'out' as she was dressed like her elder sister.

'It leads one astray; one does not know what to do. The close bonnet and demure air you describe so well... tell one what is expected; but I got into a dreadful scrape last year from the want of them... I had not a suspicion that I could be doing anything wrong. They looked just the same both well–dressed, with veils and parasols like other girls; but

I afterwards found that I had been giving all my attention to the youngest who was not out, and had most excessively offended the eldest'.

Mansfield Park

Bonnets could be made at home, however they were also readily available from milliners. Wealthy women would often get a bonnet made to complement an outfit, but for others, including the gentry of Jane Austen's novels, it was economical to redecorate a bonnet as fashion, or personal inclination, changed. As Lydia comments to her sisters in *Pride and Prejudice*, pulling apart a bonnet and trimming it with new satin ribbon could easily refresh it.

'Look here, I have bought this bonnet, I do not think it is very pretty; but I thought I might as well buy it as not. I shall pull it to pieces as soon as I get home, and see if I can make it up any better.' And when her sisters abused it as ugly, she added with perfect unconcern, 'Oh, but there are two or three more uglier in the shop; and when I have bought some prettier—coloured satin to trim it with fresh, I think it will be very tolerable'.

Pride and Prejudice

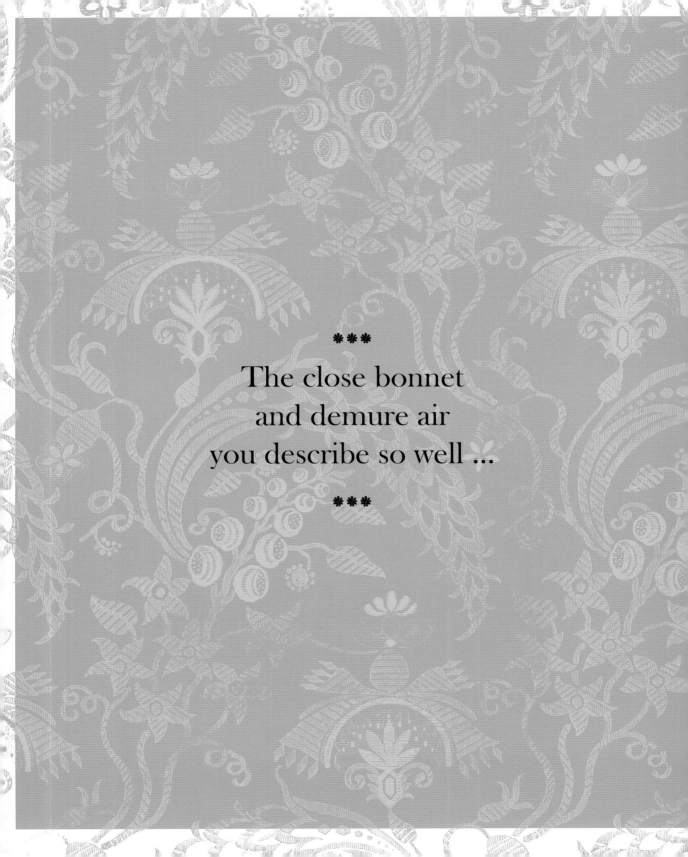

***

The close bonnet
and demure air
you describe so well ...

***

Catherine's 'new straw bonnet', which she worries about as the rain falls upon her arrival at Northanger Abbey, is a reminder that the straw bonnet provided an excellent and economical foundation for trimming and re-trimming over time. Other materials, such as fur, cotton, velvet and silk were also popular materials from which to make the crown and brim of the bonnet.

There were numerous ways to trim up a new bonnet, limited only by imagination and resources. The old trims were removed and replaced, for example at the brim, the band and on top and around the crown. Ribbons, feathers and lace were common trims. Miss Steele's hat in *Sense and Sensibility* is trimmed by her sister, Lucy.

'Look, she made me this bow to my hat, and put in the feather last night. There now, you are going to laugh at me too. But why should not I wear pink ribbons?'

Sense and Sensibility

Jewels, braids, half-veils covering the face, and fruit were also popular trims. In a letter to Cassandra Austen dated 2 June 1799, Jane Austen recounts the latest fashion trends in hat decoration.

'Flowers are very much worn & Fruit is still more the thing—Eliz has a bunch of Strawberries, & I have seen Grapes, Cherries, Plumbs & Apricots—There are likewise

Almonds & raisins, french Plumbs & Tamarinds at the Grocers, but I have not seen any of them in hats'.

The shape of a bonnet varied greatly throughout the Regency Era; from the flat straw hat with a large brim and a soft crown tied with a wide swathe of ribbon, to the close bonnet with a deep brim hiding the face, and the tall straight crown with a small brim popular later in the era.

❋ ❋ ❋

Bonnet

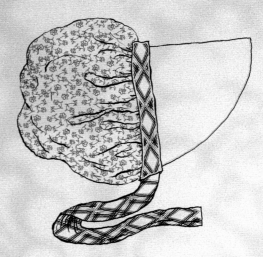

MATERIALS

* A straw hat to fit — straw sewn in strips (not blended or chipped straw)
* 1 m of thick, strong interfacing (used to line shirts and dresses)
* 1.5 m of silk, velvet or cotton
* Quilting thread
* 2.5 m of ribbon(s) for tie of varying widths
* 1 m of 1 cm wide ribbon or cord for soft decorative crown
* Feathers, lace or other items for decoration

TOOLS

* Sewing machine
* Scissors
* Tape measure
* Tracing paper
* Iron and ironing board
* Sewing needle
* Safety pins

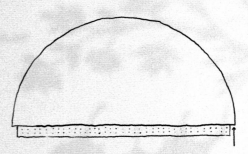

diagram 1

INSTRUCTIONS

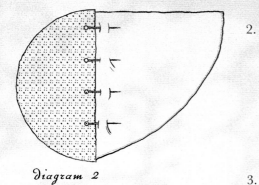

diagram 2

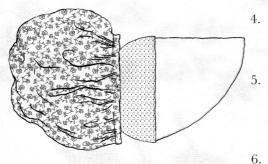

diagram 3

1. Unpick the brim of the straw hat until only the bowl shape of the crown remains. Secure the straw with a few hand stitches, using the quilting thread, to the end of the crown.

2. Measure the circumference of the crown and subtract 10 cm from the figure (e.g. a 64 cm circumference becomes 54 cm). Draw a straight line measuring the length of your final figure (e.g. 54 cm) onto a piece of tracing paper. Draw a half-circle onto this straight line. The depth of the half-circle will become the depth of the brim. A 20 cm half circle at its highest point gives a deep, close bonnet.

3. Cut out the tracing paper pattern of the brim and pin to fabric. Next, cut out two separate pieces of the fabric.

4. Pin tracing paper pattern to interfacing. Cut out one piece of interfacing. Trim 1.5 cm off long side of interfacing.

5. With wrong sides of the two fabric pieces together, sew with sewing machine or by hand around curve of brim, leaving the straight side open. Clip curves as necessary to get a smooth curve edge.

6. Turn the brim fabric right side out and iron curve.

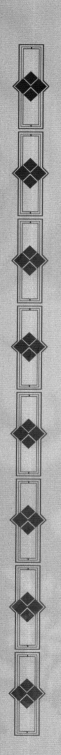

7. Insert the interfacing into brim (Diagram 1). Turn under the hem on both sides of the straight length of the brim by 1.5 cm. Iron and pin into place. Stitch straight down the length so that a neat row of stitches is visible on the joined fabric.

8. Pin brim to the straw crown, with deepest part of the brim at the top and the 10 cm gap between the two edges at the base of the crown (Diagram 2).

9. Using the quilting thread, hand sew the brim into place.

10. At this point, the brim and crown form one type of bonnet and can be decorated with ribbons. A wide strong ribbon can be stitched between the join of the brim and bonnet and tied under the chin to secure.

11. Alternatively to create a bonnet with a full, soft crown create a headpiece to fit over the crown base (Diagram 3). Using a tape measure mark a 30 cm circle onto the fabric. To mark the circle, place a cross at the centre of the fabric then, placing one end of the tape measure on the cross, mark 30 cm out around in a circle. Cut out the circle.

12. Iron and pin under a 1.5 cm hem around the circle. Stitch into place, leaving a 2 cm gap.

13. Insert the 1 cm thick ribbon on the end of a safety pin. This becomes your drawstring. Ease through the hem until the entire circle can be pulled tight into a gathered bag shape. Fluff out crown until it is as full as desired. Stitch the two ends of the ribbon into place and close the 2 cm gap in the hem.

14. Stitch the soft fabric crown onto the straw bonnet by hand using the quilting thread.

Reticule

Novels *Emma, Mansfield Park*

❀ ❀ ❀

Carrying personal items has often presented challenges for women. The bulky, voluminous skirts of the early 18th century allowed women to carry their personal items in pockets underneath their main decorative skirt. A pocket, shaped like a pear, was attached around the waist with ties or tied to a petticoat and could be decorated with embroidery. As women's fashion changed to the soft, layered and more natural dresses of the Regency Era such pockets could not be tied around the waist without leaving unsightly bulges in the line of the dress.

Reticules, also called ridicules or indispensables, replaced pockets and were held separately in the hand. The reticule held a handkerchief, smelling salts or scented water in a small bottle, letters, a pocket book (a small date book like a diary) and a coin purse (the purse was quite small—see Purses, page 85). Mrs Elton in *Emma* uses a purple and gold reticule, expensive colours that Austen possibly chose to sketch her character's pretensions to grandeur, associated as they were with royalty and luxury.

She [Emma] *soon believed herself to penetrate Mrs Elton's thoughts, and understand why she was, like herself in happy spirits; it was being in Miss Fairfax's confidence, and fancying herself acquainted with what was still a secret to other people. Emma saw symptoms of it immediately in the expression of her face… she saw her with a sort of anxious parade of mystery fold up a letter which she had apparently been reading aloud to Miss Fairfax, and return it into the purple and gold reticule by her side*

Emma

The reticule was often a round or diamond-shaped drawstring bag, that could be painted, embroidered or decorated with trimming and fringes. While the drawstring provided a simple and efficient way of closing the reticule, metal clasps could also be purchased. The intention was to make a beautiful item that both displayed skill and complemented dresses; linen, silk, velvet and soft leather were popular fabrics used to make the reticule.

Embroidery was one form of fancy work which could be worked while in company, demonstrating skill while also producing useful gifts for family and friends. While metal, silk and gold threads were used to decorate fine clothing, the high cost of such threads meant that much embroidery completed in the home used threads like wool, linen and cotton. Embroidery designs could be copied from the fashion magazines in circulation, such as *The Lady's Magazine* or *Entertaining Companion for the Fair Sex* and *La Belle Assemblee* or *Bell's Court & Fashionable Magazine Addressed Particularly to the Ladies.* Families also collected embroidery designs, worked by a family member or servant, to circulate amongst themselves. A design was either copied from a magazine or drawn directly onto paper. Ink was then used to trace the design onto the fabric. A transparent fabric like muslin could be placed directly over the paper design. For heavier fabrics, the paper design was pricked with pins, placed over the fabric and then an appropriate substance—white chalk for dark fabric or charcoal on white—was pushed through the pin pricks to give the outline of the design that was then connected by ink or a hurried outline in thread.

A knotted fringe was used to decorate embroidered items like a reticule. Lady Bertram in *Mansfield Park* is a prolific producer of fringe, as noted on Sir Thomas' return from Antigua.

But not one of the circle was he listened to with such unbroken, unalloyed enjoyment as by his wife... She had been

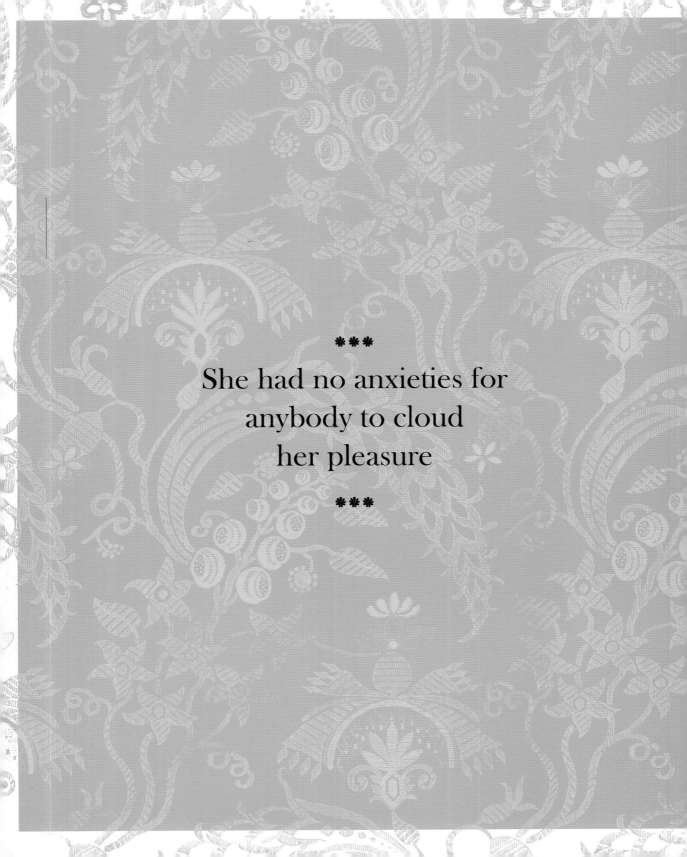

***

She had no anxieties for
anybody to cloud
her pleasure

***

almost fluttered for a few minutes, and still remained so sensibly animated as to put away her work, move Pug from her side, and give all her attention and all the rest of her sofa to her husband. She had no anxieties for anybody to cloud her pleasure; her own time had been irreproachably spent during his absence; she had done a great deal of carpet—work, and made many yards of fringe.

Mansfield Park

Using a knotting shuttle, small regular knots were tied in silk, wool or linen thread. The resulting knotted piece, or fringe, was then couched down (small stitches in a matching colour) as an outline around decoration on a dress, reticule, workbag or worked into an embroidery design.

Reticule

MATERIALS

* 50 x 25 cm of cream fabric (linen, silk, fine wool or cotton used for front embroidered panel)
* 40 cm square of fabric for base
* 50 x 25 cm of lining fabric
* 30 x 30 cm square of all-purpose woven fusible interfacing (to back embroidery)
* Linen, silk or cotton thread in three shades of pink and two shades of green (reticule in photograph uses linen thread DMC L223, L225, L760, L3103 and L 3102)
* 1 m of matching ribbon or cord for drawstring
* Sewing cotton

TOOLS

* Embroidery needle and scissors
* Embroidery hoop
* Knotting shuttle (optional)
* Sewing machine or hand sewing
* Fabric scissors
* Tape measure
* Transfer pen or pencil
* Large safety pin
* Iron

INSTRUCTIONS

1. Transfer embroidery design onto cream fabric according to transfer pen or pencil instructions.

2. Attach (iron) all purpose woven fusible interfacing to back of embroidery and place in embroidery hoop. Tighten fabric into hoop firmly.

3. Using a single strand of cream linen thread, sew over the transfer pen outline in running stitch.

4. Separate two strands of linen from the thread. Work embroidered flower in long and short stitch to give a shading effect moving out from the centre of the flower from dark to light (Diagram 2). The leaves are also worked in long and short stitch with dark green at the centre. The stems are worked in overcast stitch.

5. Remove from embroidery hoop and iron carefully.

6. Attach lining fabric to the embroidered front panel with right sides together, ironing under a 2.5 cm hem and pin into place around three sides, leave the base open. Straight stitch around three sides on the sewing machine or with back stitch by hand. Turn right way out and iron the three seams.

7. On the unstitched base side, iron under a 2.5 cm hem and pin into place. Stitch this side.

8. At the top of the panel, iron and pin down a 2.5 cm casing on the inside of the panel. This becomes the casing for the drawstring. Stitch into place.

9. Iron, pin and stitch sides of panel together to form a tube, right sides are on the inside.

10. Using the fabric for the base, cut out a 25 cm circle (the circumference is 25 cm). Stitch a small hem around the edge of the circle.

11. With the tube front panel inside out, pin the base circle (hem of circle facing up) to the base of the tube, creating small pleats around the base (Diagram 1). Stitch base into place.

12. Turn right way out. Attach safety pin to ribbon or cord and thread through the drawstring casing and secure ends of drawstring.

13. Using a knotting shuttle, make a series of evenly spaced knots in the thread, using all six strands in the thread. The thread should measure 50 cm on completion. The knotting shuttle holds the thread and assists in making the knots even, however making a series of knots in the thread can be worked without the shuttle by simply tying evenly spaced knots in the thread. With small stitches in the same colour thread, sew the knotted thread over the stitched casing edge.

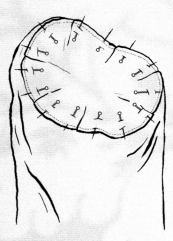

Diagram 1

Embroidery Design
Enlarge by 200%

diagram 2

193
Reticule

Technique Knitting
Level Advanced

Knitted rug

Novels *Sense and Sensibility*

The scene in *Sense and Sensibility*, when Marianne Dashwood receives a dismissive letter from Willoughby introduces a Regency tradition, the late breakfast.

'*As this was a favourite meal* [breakfast] *with Mrs Jennings, it lasted a considerable time, and they were just setting themselves, after it, round the common working table, when a letter was delivered to Marianne, which she eagerly caught from the servant, and, turning of a death—like paleness, instantly ran out of the room. Elinor, who saw as plainly by this, as if she had seen the direction* [address]*, that it must come from Willoughby, felt immediately such a sickness at heart as made her hardly able to hold her head, and sat in such a general tremor as made her fear it impossible to escape Mrs Jenning's notice...Of Elinor's distress, she was too busily employed in measuring lengths of worsted for her rug to see any thing at all'.*

Sense and Sensibility

While many workers and farmers were already at work, having eaten a solid meal of porridge, bread and maybe eggs, the middle classes were beginning their light breakfast meal at 9 or 10 am. A late breakfast echoed the fashion for increasingly later evening dinners. When Jane Austen visits Godmersham Park she writes to Cassandra in 1808 that 'It has struck ten, I must go to breakfast'. A late breakfast provided two to three hours to prepare the day's menu with the cook or housekeeper, practise the pianoforte, tend to morning chores, write letters or go shopping if staying in town.

A typical middle class breakfast included toast, butter, jam and tea—perhaps also drinking chocolate, coffee, cake and eggs. Breakfast for the aristocracy and other wealthy families was a far more elaborate event, particularly if guests were invited, with the addition of meat in many forms—kippers, herring, bacon, kidneys, sausage—to the full middle class menu.

As the London mail delivery was usually at 9 am to the door, mail and any newspapers delivered would be read at the breakfast table. Though as Marianne Dashwood had just written to Willoughby that morning and she receives a reply after breakfast, the letter may have arrived in one or other of the 2 or 3 mail runs common in London. In rural areas, mail was generally picked up directly at the post office, unless collected by servants or the extra fee paid for delivery to the door. Early morning guests, particularly nearby family or friends, also joined the breakfast table.

In smaller houses the dining room served as the breakfast room, but in many houses a smaller room, rather than a large, public dining room was set aside for the family's breakfast room. As this room was heated for breakfast, the women of the family, as do Mrs Jennings and Elinor Dashwood, used the breakfast room for the morning's sewing. The breakfast table may have been cleared or alternatively a smaller table placed by the window, for light, became the work table.

Mrs Jenning's lengths of worsted for her rug may have been worsted wool or cotton for carpetwork, crewel work or knitting. Wool was very much a staple of British agriculture and used in a wide range of crafts. Silk yarn was also used for embroidery and knitting, as was cotton yarn, which was introduced in the late 17th century. After carding worsted yarn is combed to separate the long and short fibres, leaving only the long fibres with the fibres lying parallel against each other. It is then given a slight twist when spun into yarn. As a result, worsted yarns are usually stronger, smoother, quick drying and produce a fine cloth when woven.

***

She was too busily employed
in measuring lengths of
worsted for her rug

***

Worsted cloth was particularly used for clothing in the Regency Era.

The smoothness and fine quality of worsted wool made it appropriate for carpetwork and crewel work. Carpetwork on the tough canvas grid required strong wool while crewel work, decorative stitches onto a firm linen or cotton, required the fine finish of worsted wool. Later in *Sense and Sensibility* Mrs Jennings is busy at her carpetwork, so the pieces of worsted she was measuring earlier were probably for this carpetwork rug.

Jane Austen's mother was fond of knitting, making gloves and rugs in particular. She appears to have made rugs for family and friends, including Martha Lloyd, Elizabeth Austen (brother Edward's wife) and most likely Cassandra Austen. Jane Austen conveys her mother's offer of a knitted rug to Cassandra in 1807:

'Martha's rug is just finished & looks well, tho' not quite as well as I hoped. I see no fault in the Border, but the Middle is dingy — My Mother desires me to say that she will knit one for you, as soon as you return to chuse the colours & pattern'.

The knitted rugs as gifts may have been rugs to put on a bed, beside a bed as a foot rug or as a hearth rug in front of a fire.

In the era before knitting books were published, Mrs Austen probably worked her own designs for the rugs. Sending a message through Jane in 1808, Mrs Austen directs Cassandra to a breakfast room rug for inspiration.

'She desires me to say that she does not doubt your making out the Star pattern very well, as you have the Breakfast room—rug to look at'.

As a breakfast room rug, it was probably placed in front of the fire to protect the floor from sparks.

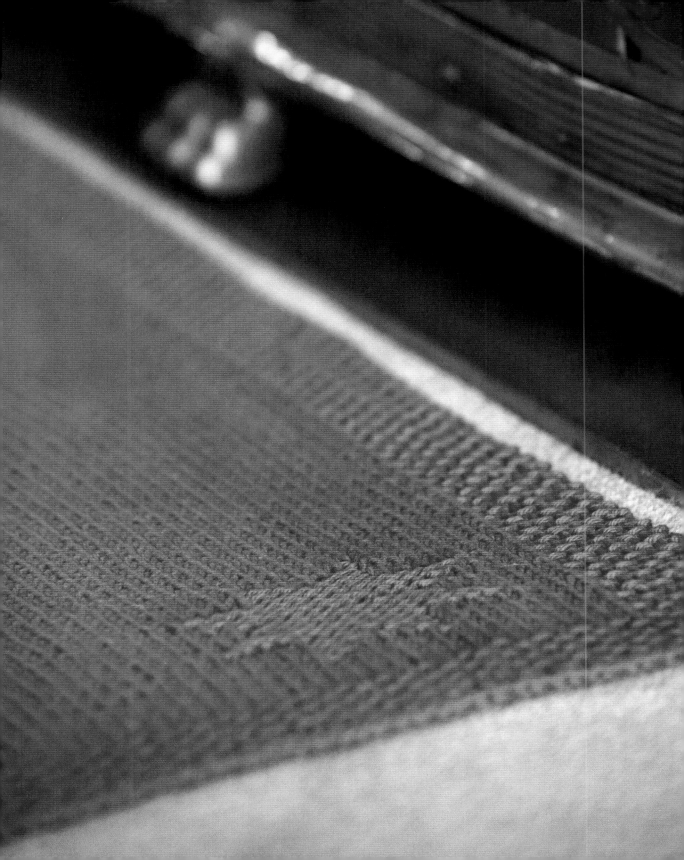

Knitted rug

Finished size: 54 x 82 cm

MATERIALS

* 2 balls of 100% pure cotton
  worsted weight (Lion Cotton used)

TOOLS

* 4 mm knitting needles

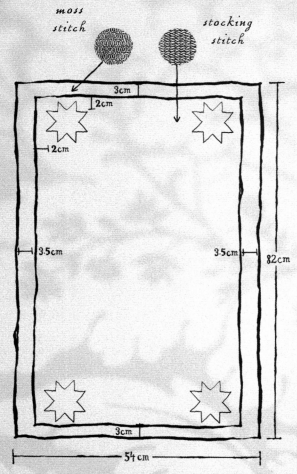

INSTRUCTIONS

1. Cast on 90 stitches.

2. Work 8 rows of moss stitch (the moss stitch forms a border on all four sides). This border measures approximately 3 cm.

3. Change to stocking stitch to make the body of the rug, while maintaining a moss stitch border at each end. The first row after the moss stitch border is: Work 8 stitches in moss stitch, work 74 stitches in stocking stitch, work 8 stitches in moss stitch. Work four rows in total (pattern abbreviated: 8MS, 74SS, 8MS).

4. Start the reverse stocking stitch star in the next row (or fifth row from border). Work 8 moss stitches, then 4 stocking stitches before commencing the first star in reverse stocking stitch—knit in reverse stocking stitch for each of the stitches marked on the star pattern. Then work 36 stocking stitches before working the second star pattern, then 4 stocking stitches and finish the row with 8 moss stitches. Repeat until star pattern is finished (pattern abbreviated: 8MS, 4SS, 15 Star RSS, 36SS, 15 Star RSS, 4SS, 8MS).

5. Resume pattern of working 8 moss stitches, 74 stocking stitches and finishing with 8 moss stitches (pattern abbreviated: 8MS, 74SS, 8MS). Work 145 rows in this pattern until the piece measures 72 cm from casting on.

6.   Repeat step four to work in the star patterns.

7.   Work 4 rows of the main pattern: 8 moss stitch, 74 stocking stitch, 8 moss stitch (pattern abbreviated: 8MS, 74SS, 8MS).

8.   Finish with 8 rows of moss stitch to form the final border and cast off.

9.   Blocking the rug will smooth out the wrinkles made through knitting. To block the finished rug, fill washing machine or basin with cold water and soak rug until cotton is thoroughly saturated. Spin out water.

10.   Lay rug on a flat surface, ensuring it is laid out in shape. Pull into shape if needed.

11.   When dry, finish with a steam iron.

STOCKING STITCH (SS)

Row 1: Knit (Right side)
Row 2: Purl (Wrong side)
Repeat Row 1, then Row 2 and so on.

REVERSE STOCKING STITCH: (RSS)

Row 1: Purl
Row 2: Knit
That is: Reverse the pattern—purl on a right side or knit row, then knit on a wrong side or purl row.

MOSS STITCH (MS)

In multiple of two stitches
Row 1: Knit 1, Purl 1
Row 2: As row 1

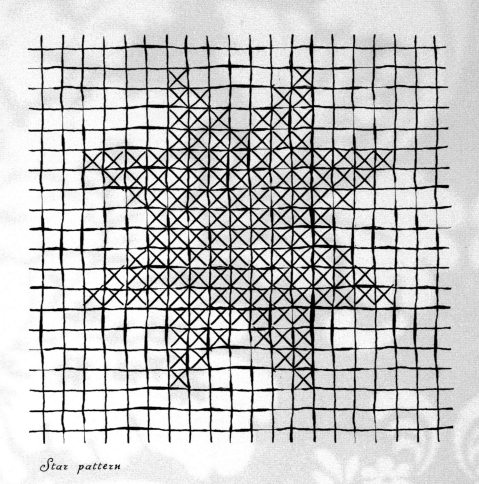

Star pattern

207
Knitted rug

Muslin cap

Novels *Northanger Abbey, Emma*

❊ ❊ ❊

During the Regency Era, covering the hair with either a bonnet outside, or a cap inside, was necessary for both social and practical reasons. While it was common for married or older women to wear a cap inside, all women were expected to wear a bonnet or hat outside. A cap would often be placed under the bonnet for warmth. A cap also served important practical reasons inside the house. In houses that were not heated to the warm temperatures of modern life, a cap retained warmth and complemented the other accessories used to keep warm, such as shawls and fingerless gloves.

Jane Austen appreciated the cap for another practical reason—it allowed her to hide her hair under the cap with minimal fuss. In a letter to Cassandra Austen on 1 December 1798 Jane comments;

'...I have made myself two or three caps to wear of evenings since I came home, and they save me a world of torment as to hairdressing, which at present gives me no trouble beyond washing and brushing, for my long hair is always plaited up out of sight, and my short hair curls well enough to want no papering'.

Caps were usually worn in the morning, being replaced for dinner (which could be anywhere from mid-afternoon to late evening) by more elaborate caps, decorated with feathers, ribbons and lace, or turbans.

Caps were white and made from muslin, cotton or linen. Muslin was the fabric of choice during the Regency Era and as Henry Tilney demonstrates, in conversation on first meeting Mrs Allen and Catherine in Northanger Abbey, caps could be easily made from cast-off muslin dress material.

'Do you understand muslins, sir?'
'Particularly well, I always buy my own cravats, and am allowed to be an excellent judge, and my sister has often trusted me in the choice of a gown. I brought one for her

the other day and it was pronounced to be a prodigious bargain by every lady who saw it. I gave but five shillings a yard for it, and a true Indian muslin'.

Mrs Allen was quite struck by his genius 'Men commonly take so little notice of those things' said she 'I can never get Mr Allen to notice one of my gowns from another. You must be a great comfort to your sister, sir'.

'I hope I am madam'.

'And pray, sir what do you think of Miss Morland's gown?'

'It is very pretty, madam' said he, gravely examining it, 'but I do not think it will wash well, I am afraid it will fray.'

'how can you be' said Catherine laughing 'be so ———' she had almost said strange.

'I am quite of the opinion, sir' replied Mrs Allen 'and so I told Miss Morland when she brought it'.

'But then you know madam, muslin always turns to some account or other, Miss Morland will get enough out of it for a handkerchief, or a cap, or a cloak. Muslin can never be said to be wasted. I have heard my sister say so forty times, when she has been extravagant in buying more than she wanted, or careless in cutting it to pieces.'

Northanger Abbey

Muslin cap

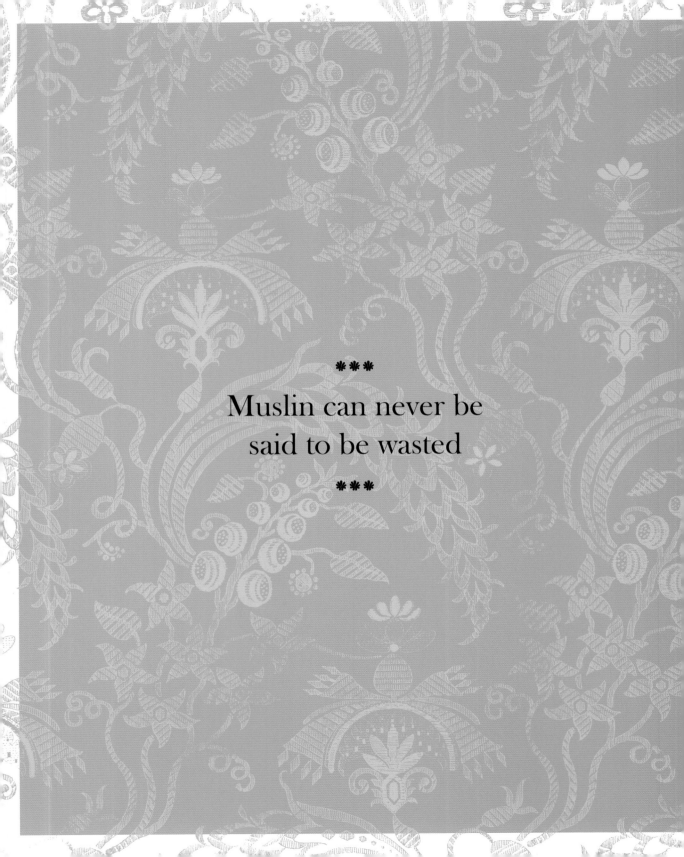

***

Muslin can never be
said to be wasted

***

The popularity of muslin, and other cottons, reflected the consolidation of trade with India and the growth of cotton mills within Britain. Muslin was prized for the soft gentle lines that the open, transparent and soft weave creates. It allowed a simpler natural fashion to emerge, modelled on classical lines inspired by ancient Rome and Greece. Yards of muslin in multiple layers were required to make a dress, with an underdress of stronger fabric such as a linen or silk, and petticoats were also required for modesty.

Caps could also be made out of lace, with the traditional lace making areas of Italy, Flanders (Belgium) and France providing much of the lace available in Britain. The high cost of obtaining this lace and the delicate nature of lace meant that only the wealthy, leisured class of women would wear a lace cap. However, muslin decorated with embroidery, particularly whitework, white thread on white fabric, resembles the transparent and delicate nature of lace and was a popular way to decorate caps.

As with other needlework performed by women, construction and decoration of caps also demonstrated skill, which is seen in *Emma* when Miss Bates shows off new caps and new workbags. While it was possible to purchase a range of pre-made clothing items from shops during the Regency Era, it is more likely that Miss Bates made these at home out of cast-off material.

Muslin cap

Finished size—make to fit

MATERIALS

* 50 x 115 cm piece of white muslin
* 1.5 m of ribbon and lace—multiple
  lengths of each required for decoration
* 80 cm white cotton cord (becomes drawstring)
* 80 cm white bias binding (approx. 2 cm wide)
* Tracing paper
* Reel of sewing thread in matching colour

TOOLS

* Fabric scissors
* Tape measure
* Pins
* Sewing machine
  (can also be made by hand)
* Pencil

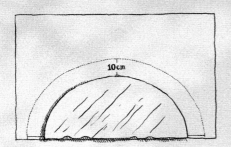

Diagram 1

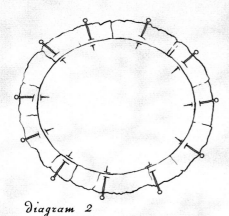

Diagram 2

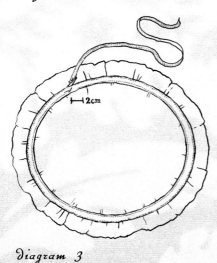

Diagram 3

INSTRUCTIONS

1. Measure your head from brow to mid-back and add 2.5 cm for a seam allowance.

2. Measure your head from 2 cm above the left ear to 2 cm above the right ear. Then add 2.5 cm for a seam allowance.

3. Taking your measurements, draw a cross on a large piece of tracing paper—the vertical axis is the first measurement you took and the horizontal axis is the second measurement.

4. Connect the four segments of your cross with a pencil to make it an oval shape. This forms the pattern for the crown of your cap. Cut out.

5. To make a pattern for the brim, fold the crown pattern in half and lay on tracing paper. Using your tape measure and pencil draw a 10 cm half circle shape around the crown (Diagram 1). Marking the 10 cm distance every 5 cm around the half circle will help keep the pattern even. Cut out.

6. Pin crown pattern to muslin and cut out.

7. Pin brim pattern to muslin. Cut the brim on a fold to create a full circle when cut.

219
Muslin cap

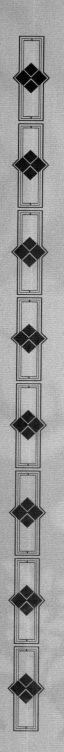

8. Pin brim to crown by easing it around the crown, it should create a few small tucks (Diagram 2). Then sew brim to crown with a sewing machine or by hand, using backstitch.

9. Turn muslin piece wrong side up and pin on bias binding over the join. Sew down both sides of the bias binding, leaving a 2 cm opening in which to thread your drawstring.

10. Using a safety pin, thread your drawstring through the bias binding casing (Diagram 3). Pull drawstring in so that a full crown is made and test on your head for desired gathered look and size.

11. Secure the two ends of the drawstring together with a few stitches. Sew up the 2 cm opening in the casing.

12. Now hem the edge of your brim with whitework embroidery or ribbons and lace.

13. Decorate the rest of the cap as you wish. You may like to cover over the casing with ribbon.

Acknowledgements

I would like to thank the following craftspeople for their contribution to this book:

The netting for the coin purse (page 84) was made by Rita Bartholomew. Rita Bartholomew lives in Massachusetts, USA and pursues many craft interests, with a particular love for netting. The skill of netting was passed down to Rita by her grandmother, who had in turn learnt the art from her Swedish mother. With many years of experience in netting, Rita designs and nets a range of items as well as creating and documenting netting stitches, which she shares with others at her website, www.knotsindeed.com.

Marlena De Mars made the painted glass Transparency on page 154. Her interests include cross-stitch, photography, scrapbooking, jewellery, sewing and glass painting. Initially inspired by Ancient Egypt, her art now reflects themes and styles from different eras and nations.

Suzanne Bollard designed and knitted the hearth rug featured on page 194. Suzanne lives in Australia and pursues a wide range of creative crafts including quilting, appliqué and beading. Knitting is her true passion. As a highly experienced, quality knitter she has designed and knitted a range of items over the years.

I would also like to thank Anne Kelly from the National Museum of Australia who shared her passion for the Regency and the museum's collection with me.

All quotes from Jane Austen's letters are drawn from Le Faye, D (ed.) 1995, *Jane Austen's Letters*, 2nd edn, Oxford University Press, Oxford, pp. 5, 7, 22, 24, 42, 53, 77, 117, 118, 126, 141, 142, 187. Reprinted by permission.

Image Credits: Ackermann's Costume Plates: pages 37, 51, 67, 77, 93, 107, 119, 131, 145, 171, 175, 185, 213; corbis: page 199; Getty images: page 3; Photolibrary / Bridgeman Art Library: pages 6-7, 22-23, 30-31, 40, 80-81, 88-89,108, 121, 134, 148,159, 189, 202, 216, 221.

List of Suppliers

* Rice and other papers for craft: Dawnandra Crafts, www.dawnandracrafts.com.au
* Netting patterns and instructions: Knots Indeed, www.knotsindeed.com
* Tools, kits and supplies including netting kits and instructions: Lacis, www.lacis.com
* Metal clasps, buttons, ribbons, books and patterns: Ortensia Sewing Supplies, www.ortensia.com.au
* Reproductions of historic fabrics, including Regency Era: Reproduction Fabrics, www.reproductionfabrics.com
* Purse patterns and frames: The Quilting Heart & Studio Mia, www.thequiltingheart.com
* Eighteenth & nineteenth century fabrics, patterns and sewing tools: W.M. Booth Draper, www.wmboothdraper.com